# Quick & Easy

# TAPAS FROM JAPAN

## POPULAR " IZAKAYA " RECIPES

OVERSEAS DISTRIBUTORS
UNITED STATES:JP TRADING,INC.
      400 Forbes Blvd., Unit 3
      South San Francisco, CA 94080
      Phone:(650)871-3940
      Fax:(650)871-3944
MEXICO:Editorial Sayrols, S.A.de C. V.
COLOMBIA:Jorge E.Morales & CIA.LTDA.
TAIWAN: Formosan Magazine Press, Ltd.
HONG KONG :Apollo Book Company, Ltd.
THAILAND:Central Department Store Ltd.
SINGAPORE: MPH DISTRIBUTORS(S)PTE, LTD.
MALAYSIA:MPH DISTRIBUTORS SDN, BHD.
PHILIPPINES:National Book Store, Inc.
KOREA:Tongjin Chulpan Muyeok Co., Ltd.
INDONESIA: TOKO BUKU HARAPAN
INDIA:Dani BooK Land, Bombay 14
AUSTRALIA:BOOKWISE INTERNATIONAL
GUAM,SAIPAN AND MICRONESIAN ISLANDS:FUJIWARA'S SALES & SERVICE
CANADA:MILESTONE PUBLICATIONS
U.S.A.:MASA T.& ASSOCIATES
U.S.A.:A.K.HARANO COMPANY
HAWAII:HAKUBUNDO,INC

Original Copyrigh© 2000   Boutique-sha
World rights reserved.Published by JOIE,INC.1-8-3,Hirakawa-cho, Chiyoda-ku, Tokyo 102-0093 Japan      Printed in Hong Kong
No part of this book or portions thereof may be reproduced in any form or by any means including electoronic retrieval systems without prior written approval from the author or publisher.
ISBN4-915831-88-4

# FOREWORD

This book is an introduction to Japanese tapas or small dishes served at Tokyo's most popular pubs today. Japanese pubs called "*izakaya*" used to be small drinking stalls exclusively for men in the Edo period, but are rapidly becoming an urban oasis for not only male but female business people who seek real gourmet food along with good beverages. *Izakaya* proudly serve signature variations of many popular dishes, unlike most formal Japanese restaurants.

This practically illustrated cookbook includes about 120 recipes which reveal the chefs' secrets that everyone wants to know, for dishes ranging from the traditional "grandma's favorite" to trendy snack.

All of the recipes are adjustable and can be served in small portions as appetizers or in large batches for parties. Some ingredients and seasonings might sound unfamiliar to you, especially in the first section entitled "Typical *Izakaya* Dishes". Most of them are readily available in Oriental food stores, but, be creative using ingredients on hand, referring the Glossary on page 92 to 95.

On top of every page, you will find a heading such as "Light Meals" or "Quick Appetizers", which suggests resulting volume and cooking time so that you can choose the most suitable dishes as you flip through the pages.

Recipes are illustrated step by step for easy understanding. The numbers of pictures shows how each step should be done and adds useful hints. Since the recipes are supposed to be served in a small portion to have with alcoholic drinks, they are often strongly seasoned. Adjust the amount of salt if you prefer milder taste.

Tapas from Japan not only includes dishes originated in Japan, but also in Korea, China, or Italy, which have long been fitted into Japanese taste buds, some in their authentic styles, others in adapted forms. In order to suggest the origins, we have reserved the original language as often as possible.

Authentic Japanese dishes have titles both in English and original (in parentheses) so you can make an order next time you go into one of the *izakaya* .

Now, enjoy these savory, healthy, and easy-to-make dishes.

# CONTENTS

# BASIC MEASUREMENTS

1 teaspoon (tsp) = 5 ml
1 tablespoon (Tbsp) =15 ml
1 cup = 240 ml

## Weight converted from volume

| | Level Measurements | | |
| --- | --- | --- | --- |
| | 1 tsp | 1 Tbsp | 1 cup |
| water,vinegar,*sake* | 5 g | 15 g | 240 g |
| soy sauce, *mirin*, *miso* | 6 g | 18 g | 288 g |
| salt | 5 g | 15 g | 240 g |
| sugar(granulated) | 3 g | 9 g | 144 g |

Sometimes it is simpler to estimate quantities by eye/hand measurements.Here are some practical gauges for such approximate measurements.

## Hand measurements of salt
1 handful = 3 Tbsp
1 fistful = 2 Tbsp
1 pinch (with 3 fingers) = 1/2 tsp
1 pinch (with 2 fingers) = 1/4 tsp

## Eye measurements of vegetables
1 medium carrot, 4"(10 cm )long = 7 oz (200 g)
1 medium Chinese cabbage = 4 1/2 lb (2 kg)
1 Japanese-type cucumber = 3 1/2 oz (100 g)
1 Japanese-type  eggplant = 3 1/2 oz (100g)
1 medium turnip = 3 1/2 oz (100g)
1 thumb-size ginger root = 1/3 oz (10 g)

## Converting from U.S.customary system

● **Liquid Measures**
1 cup = 16Tbsp = 8 oz =236 ml (240 ml)

● **Weights**
grams $\times$ 0.035 = ounces
ounces $\times$ 28.35 = grams

● **Linear Measures**
inches $\times$ 2.54 = cetimeters
centimeters $\times$ 0.39 =inches

● **Temperatures**
C = (F - 32) $\times$ 5/9

$$F = \frac{C \times 9}{5} + 32$$

C = Celsius
F = Fahrenheit

### Deep-frying oil temperatures
300°F -330°F (150°C -165°C) = low
340°F -350°F (170°C -175°C) = moderate(medium)
350°F -360°F (175°C -180°C) = high

# WHAT IS *IZAKAYA?*

### *Izakaya* in the Past

For hundreds of years, Japanese style taverns called *izakaya*, have existed as hideaways for the ordinary workers and townspeople on the journey home after a hard day. They needed "a stepping stone" or two, to refresh themselves, or to "blow away" the day's worries by chatting with coworkers over *sake* and nibbles served at affordable prices.

These "cheap" drinking establishments including shabby roofed stalls on wheels called "*yatai*", were recognizable by special signs such as a red lantern (*aka-chochin*), or a cotton or hemp-rope curtain (*noren* or *nawa-noren*) at the entrance. At those places you didn't have to worry about unreasonable bills which could instantly sober one up.

### What You Can Find Beyond "*Noren*"

The *noren* is a curtain printed with the shop's name on it and is used to signal whether they are open or not. If the curtain is hung just outside the entrance, they are open. If the curtain is hung behind the wooden doors, they are closed.

The word "*noren*" acts as much more than just a screen. "*Noren*" can be found in quite a few expressions of japanrese, not only as a symbol at the entrance of a shop, but also to substantiate the credit, reputation or even goodwill of the shop: *Noren wo kuguru*, or go under *noren*, means to go for a drink: *Noren wo wakeru*, or sharing it, means to give a business license to an employee: *Noren wo kegasu*, or soiling it, to impair the credit of the store.

Another important feature in *izakaya* is a sliding door just behind the *noren*. Research has proved that the door of this type is used in 90% of the traditional *izakaya* in Japan, whereas only 1% of Japanese restaurants in Los Angeles are equipped with this type of door. This is an interesting contrast when you think about the nature of the Japanese people.

A major point of interest about this door is that you can "hesitate" before deciding whether or not to enter the shop, since the a narrow opening or the sliding door allows the potential customer to peek into the interior. Besides, the hanging *noren* allows you to lower your head in order to see how the inside looks and you can still close the door without letting the master see your face.

On the other hand, it seems to Japanese that the western type of hinged door requires a definite decision before you open it. This behavior might hint at the shyness of Japanese people, or the structural difference of the language, while an English sentence locates a verb followed right after a subject, in Japanese the verb is positioned at the end of a sentence. This order suggests that the Japanese language allows us some time to put off the conclusion to the last minute.

Entrance of common *izakaya*.
Before you enter, you can check out he foods and prices at the show window where intricately crafted samples are neatly displayed. *Noren* seems to be inviting you.

Entrance of new type of *izakaya*, popular among the young.

## *Izakaya* Today

The price does not seem to be the only reason why *izakaya* became so popular. Most *izakaya* patrons needed something to nibble on with their favorite beverages, and digestive light meals afterwards. These foods are called *sakana* or *tsumami*, and each *izakaya* owner/chef shows his skill by preparing delicious and/or original dishes that would satisfy both the taste buds and the wallets of his customers.

The image of *izakaya* has been completely modernized by the surprising increase in female workers as customers. As women have begun to reach higher positions in the work force, so they begun to occupy more space in the *izakaya*, both traditional and ethnic varieties. In the last ten years, women have realized that they also need a place to relax after work, rather than cooking for themselves when they get home.

After working all day they choose the inexpensive *izakaya* instead of fancy restaurants that they use for business. It was quite natural that female customers require good food to be served in a pleasant atmosphere, and the shops had to update in both software and hardware to please them. Not only the locals but foreign business people who come and stay at luxurious hotels have discovered the cozy atmosphere in the center of the city, where inexpensive but appetizing small dishes such as *yakitori* (grilled chicken skewers), *oden* (winter hot pot), or *nikujaga* (stewed beef and potatoes) are served with a variety of alcoholic beverages.

Thus, *izakaya*, which for centuries were supposed to be the domain of men, especially middle-aged workers, have begun to be shared with the other gender and another generation in a very short period of time, because of their food. In the last 5-6 years, many *izakaya* chains have been established all over the country, some of them have even extended the business to the west coast of U.S. and are gradually gaining popularity.

The category of *izakaya* has also enlarged from the traditional one to modernized spaces where Italian, Chinese, or other ethnic tapas dishes can be tasted in a small amount so that you can try a bit of everything in an informal atmosphere.

In summer, "Beer Gardens", which usually open on the rooftops of buildings, can be identified as an *izakaya*, and the customers order a variety of food, from chilled *tofu* to steaming pizza or dim sum. You will even see a variety of *izakaya* aimed at families in local towns. Some of them create a nostalgic mood of ordinary living room of the 60's, using sepia shades. Some make one a feel as if he/she is on a fishing boat. In such places, each family can enjoy numerous kinds of small dishes such as *sushi*, salads or pastas.

## Why *Izakaya* Food Gained Popularity

Owners of *izakaya* are keen on creating their own specialties along with the regular dishes, trying hard to be a different from other establishments. They try very hard to have regulars who stable the business but are price-and taste-conscious at the same time. For this reason, you can enjoy popular dishes with unique twists that might make you feel like cooking at home.

Behind the counter, Japanese cooks prepare to your special order, or serve the prepared dishes displayed on the counter in a small portion upon request.

Tables for 4-5 people are also available in *izakaya* , where a wide variety of alcoholic and nonalcoholic beverages are served along with your favorite tapas dishes.

# WHAT IS *IZAKAYA*?

Master of *izakaya* loves talks with his customers about wines and Italian cuisine, and he may call out *"Okaerinasai* (Welcome home)!" as you enter the shop the next time.

*Izakaya* with a taste of Italy, where groups of women can relax and enjoy casual conversations tasting a bit of each gourmet dish made of real ingredients.

# TYPICAL
# *IZAKAYA DISHES*

Note 1: Green onion and ginger root are essential for preparing meats as they remove odor and improve flavor. Also used in "BEEF AND POTATOES" (see p.13) or "STEWED BEEF JAPANESE STYLE" (see p.38) to enhance the flavor of meat.

# STEWED PORK *(Buta Kaku-ni)*

Enjoy this well-balanced combination of richly flavored meat, greens and rice cakes.

## Serves: 4

14 oz (400g) pork rib
7 cups water
1/2 cup *sake*
1 stalk green onion
Ginger peel
3 rice cakes
3-4 stalks *komatsuna* greens
3 1/2 Tbsp sugar
1/2 cup *mirin*
1/2 cup soy sauce
Hot mustard paste

**1** Cut pork into about 2"(5cm) squares and tie each crisscross with cotton thread. In a saucepan, bring measured water to a boil and add pork. Bring to another boil and remove scum.
**2** Add *sake*, green onion and ginger. Simmer about 2 hours, removing scum frequently.
**3** When liquid is decreased to the level that and surfaces of meat show above it, add sugar and *mirin*. Simmer a further 30 minutes.
**4** Add soy sauce and cook another 30 minutes.
**5** Boil greens and blanch in cold water. Squeeze out moisture and cut into bite-size pieces.
**6** Grill rice cakes until soft and lightly browned.
**7** Place pork, rice cakes and greens nicely on a serving dish. Serve with a dab of hot mustard paste.

Note 2: There is a golden rule to the order of adding seasonings when simmering food. First add sugar, then *mirin*, and lastly soy sauce. This way ingredients become tender first and easily absorb flavors.

**Bind each cube with cotton thread so it keeps shape.**

**Save green onion leaves and ginger root peels, and add them to remove odor of meat.**

**When liquid reduces to this height, add sugar and** *mirin*.

**Do not add soy sauce until cooked for half an hour with sugar and** *mirin*.

# COLD CUTTLEFISH

## Serves: 4

1/4 lb (120 g) cuttlefish
4 oz (120 g) baby broccoli
4" (10cm) *udo* or celery
**Miso Dressing**
> 2 oz (60 g) *saikyo miso*
> (white bean paste)
> 1 Tbsp rice vinegar
> 1 Tbsp *dashi* stock
> 1 Tbsp *tamago no moto* (see p.27)
> 1 Tbsp hot mustard paste

*Akame-tade*, optional

**1** Prepare baby broccoli as shown.
**2** Cut according to toughness as shown. In lightly salted boiling water, cook baby broccoli only briefly, tougher stems first, then flowers and leaves. Plunge into cold water, and squeeze out moisture.
**3** Skin cuttlefish and make fine, crisscross scores over surface; cut into 1" (2.5cm) wide rectangles.
**4** In boiling water, blanch cuttlefish pieces and plunge into cold water.

**5** Peel and slice *udo* or celery into thin rectangles. Soak *udo* in water 10 minutes and drain. Combine *miso* dressing ingredients and mix until smooth.
**6** In a serving dish, arrange greens, cuttlefish and *udo* slices, and pour *miso* dressing over. Garnish with *akame-tade*, if desired.

**Note**: Do not overcook baby broccoli. Take out when water along edges of pot gets bubbly.

Cut greens into 3 or 4. Make a deep slit into tough end of stalk.

Separate leaves. Adjust cooking time by adding leaves and flowers when stalks become tender.

**3**

Make decorative scores over cuttlefish so it holds dressing well.

# STEAMED CLAMS

## Serves: 4

1 lb (450 g) baby clams
3 1/2 oz (100g) *shimeji* mushrooms
1/2 cup *sake*
1/3 cup water
1/2 tsp salt
1 Tbsp butter
Scallion

**1** Prepare clams. Place clams in a colander and put in a bowl filled with salty water, as shown right. This way, clams will not swallow grains of sand they let out.
**2** Wash shells, rubbing against each other, and drain.
**3** Separate mushrooms into segments. Slice scallions thinly.
**4** In a medium pot, put clams and mushrooms. Pour in *sake*, water and salt. Cover and turn on heat.
**5** When shells are open, add butter and heat through.
**6** Transfer to a serving bowl and sprinkle with shredded scallion.

**Note**: Since overcooking makes the flesh tough, remove from heat as soon as clams are cooked.

### Preparation

Soak in salted water to remove sand from clams. Let stand at least 1 hour.

# BEEF AND POTATOES (*Nikujaga*)

## Serves: 4

10 oz (300g) beef brisket
4 medium potatoes
5 stalks green onion (or scallion)

(A) { 4 cups water
    { ½ cup *sake*
    { Ginger root, green onion

3 Tbsp sugar
1/2 cup *mirin*
1/2 cup soy sauce
1 bulb garlic
1 pod dried chili pepper
1 tsp kochu jang
    (Korean hot bean paste)
1 tsp sesame oil

**1** Peel potatoes and cut into halves or quarters.
**2** Soak potatoes in water to remove any harsh taste.
**3** Slice beef into 1/4" (6mm) thicknesses.

**4** In a medium pot, cook beef in (A) for 30-40 minutes over low heat. Add potatoes, sugar and *mirin* and continue to simmer until liquid reduces by half.
**5** Add garlic cloves, chili pepper, soy sauce and kochu jang, and simmer until flavor is absorbed by potatoes. Stir in sesame oil and remove from heat.
**6** Blanch green onion in boiling water, plunge into cold water, and squeeze out water. In a serving dish, arrange potatoes, beef and green onions.

**Note**: *Nikujaga* is one of the grandma's favorites which make people feel at home even outside their real homes. This is a spicy version, with a touch of Korean flavor.

**Trim cut edges to maintain the shape while simmering.**

**Soak potatoes in water 20-30 minutes so as to remove harsh taste and also to retain the shapes.**

You can add onions, thickly sliced, in Step 4, to further enrich the flavor.

**Slice beef into 1/4" (6mm) thicknesses.**

# *TERIYAKI* CHICKEN WITH RADISH

### Serves: 4

10 oz (300 g) chicken thigh, cut up
1/2 cup grated *daikon* radish
4" (10 cm) green onion, sliced
3 Tbsp soy sauce
3 Tbsp *mirin*
1 Tbsp sugar
Cornstarch for dusting
Vegetable oil for frying

**1** Dust chicken pieces with cornstarch. Pan-fry chicken until golden brown on both sides.

**2** While frying chicken, heat soy sauce, *mirin* and sugar in a small saucepan until thickened.

**3** Pour the thickened sauce over chicken, and remove from heat immediately to prevent scorching. Turn over chicken so all sides of chicken are coated evenly.

**4** Garnish with grated *daikon* and sprinkle with sliced green onion.

Be sure to heat through chicken before adding sauce ingredients.

Grated *daikon* radish adds a contrasting flavor to chicken and sharpens your appetite.

# FRIED MOUNTAIN YAM *(Yamaimo Isobe-age)*

### Serves: 4

10 oz (300 g) *yamatoimo* yam
3 sheets *nori* seaweed
Pinch salt
Vegetable oil for deep-frying

**1** Peel *yamatoimo* yam and grate, using a fine grater.
**2** Cut full sized *nori* into 8.
**3** Heat oil to 340°F (170°C). Spoon a small portion of grated yam onto a piece of *nori*, an deep-fry, yam side down. When the yam becomes swollen and golden, drain oil.
**4** Sprinkle with salt and serve while hot and crispy outside.

**Note**: Mountain yam (*yama-imo*) has several varieties. Do not choose *nagaimo* for frying; its moisture will splash apart. *Yamatoimo* has more speckles and whitish skin.

**Selecting the right yam**

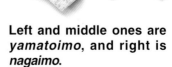

**Left and middle ones are *yamatoimo*, and right is *nagaimo*.**

Spoon on yam and immediately deep-fry each. Shown left is a bad example with shrunk *nori*.

14

**How to drain *tofu*:**

# DEEP-FRIED *TOFU* (*Agedashi -tofu*)

## Serves: 4

1 cake *tofu*
2 Japanese-type eggplants
1 2/3 cup *dashi* stock
4 Tbsp *mirin*
4 Tbsp soy sauce
2/3 cups grated *daikon* radish
3 1/3 oz (100 g) *nameko* mushrooms
1/2 bunch *mitsuba* (trefoil)
Vegetable oil for deep-frying

**1** Drain *tofu*: wrap with a kitchen cloth as shown, then roll with a bamboo mat. Place it on a flat surface and put on a weight, such as a bowl filled with water. Let stand about 30 minutes and cut into 8.
**2** Cut *mitsuba* into 1" (2.5 cm) lengths; set aside.
**3** Heat ample oil to 350°F (180°C). Dust *tofu* pieces with cornstarch and deep-fry until golden. Be sure that they don't stick to each other.
**4** Split eggplants lengthwise, and score crisscross over skin side. Cut into halves and deep-fry in 350°F (180°C) oil.

**5** In a saucepan heat *dashi*, *mirin* and soy sauce to a boil. Add mushrooms, then grated *daikon*. When the liquid starts bubbling, add *mitsuba* and remove from heat.
**6** In a serving bowl, place drained *tofu* and eggplant. Pour over the sauce.

**Note 1**: To make the outside crisp, dust 1 piece of tofu at a time before deep-frying. If not, cornstarch will absorb moisture and become soggy when fried.
**Note 2**: Try other mushrooms such as *enokidake* or *shimeji*.

Add *mitsuba* when sauce becomes bubbly along sides of pan.

---

# BEEF YANAGAWA STYLE

## Serves: 4

1/2 lb (230g) beef sirloin, sliced
3 1/2 oz (100 g) *ne-mitsuba*
2 eggs, beaten
1 2/3 cups *dashi* stock
1/4 cup *mirin*
1/4 cup soy sauce

**1** Wash *ne-mitsuba* thoroughly as shown. Cut into 1" (2.5cm) lengths.
**2** In a saucepan heat *dashi*, *mirin* and soy sauce to a boil and add *mitsuba* and beef.
**3** When beef is half cooked, drizzle in beaten eggs in a swirling motion .
**4** When eggs are nearly set, transfer to a serving dish.

**Note 1**: *Yanagawa-nabe* is a winter delicacy using small freshwater fish with burdock. Its origin is obscure, some say it is a specialty of Yanagawa, name of a restaurant in the Edo period, and some say Yanagawa is the place of the special fish. Today it seems that Yanagawa stands for a cooking method using eggs as a final touch.
**Note 2**: *Ne-mitsuba* may have soil between leaves.
**Note 3**: Try with various other ingredients such as pork, bamboo shoot, green onion, etc.

**Wash this type of *mitsuba* carefully, fanning out stem bases.**

**Drizzle in beaten eggs before beef is completely cooked. This way beef stays tender.**

Coarsely chop shrimp and fish.

# STUFFED *SHIITAKE* (*Shiitake Shinjo-age*)

### Serves: 4

8 plump *shiitake* mushrooms
1/4 lb (120 g) shrimp
1/4 lb (120 g) sablefish
3 Tbsp minced onion
Pinch salt
3 Tbsp *tamago no moto* (see p.27)
Flour for dusting
Vegetable oil for deep-frying
4 leaves green lettuce
1/2 lemon

**1** Mince shrimp and sablefish finely as shown at top.
**2** Mix them and pound into paste using back of knife .
**3** Sprinkle minced onion with salt, let stand a while, and squeeze out moisture.
**4** Mix squeezed onion with shrimp and fish paste until sticky with a kneading motion. Add

*tamago no moto* and mix well.
**5** Cut off stems of *shiitake* mushrooms. Make a crisscross cut through cap as shown.
**6** Lightly dust white sides of mushrooms with flour. Fill with fish paste and press down firmly. Coat whole mushrooms with flour.
**7** Press the center of stuffing to make a hollow so as to heat through, and deep-fry.
**8** Drain oil and serve on lettuce leaves, accompanied by lemon wedges.

**Note 1**: *Shinjo* stands for steamed or deep-fried seafood paste mixed with *yamaimo* (mountain yam) and egg white. Its delicate flavor and springy texture is prized among gourmets.

Using the back of knife, repeat "pounding and mixing" until well blended.

Sprinkle minced onion with salt and squeeze out moisture.

Using your fingers, blend seafood paste and minced onion until sticky.

Make a crisscross cut through each cap.

Fill any gap along edges of mushroom cap and press down firmly.

# VINEGARED CRAB *(Kani Sunonomo)*

### Serves: 4

1 3/4 oz (50 g) *kuzukiri*
4 oz (120 g) crabmeat
4 shallots

**Mustard Dressing**

- 1/3 cup rice vinegar
- 1 Tbsp sugar
- 1 Tbsp light soy sauce
- 1/2 Tbsp hot mustard paste

**1** Cook *kuzukiri* in boiling water for 5 minutes, constantly stirring so as not to stick each other; do not discard water and let steam 15 minutes.

**2** Shred shallots and soak in cold water until crisp.

**3** Combine seasonings for dressing.

**4** In a serving bowl, place *kuzukiri* and shredded shallots. Top with crabmeat and pour over dressing.

**Shallot**: This recipe uses young shallots harvested when the white stems are still tender.

Use cooked *kuzukiri* while transparent. It turns white after some time, in which case, blanch in boiling water again.

# SWEET SOUR CHICKEN

### Serves: 4

3/4 lb (350 g) chicken thigh
   Salt and *sake* to season
Cornstarch for dusting
Vegetable oil for deep-frying
1/2 stalk green onion
2 knobs ginger root

**Sweet and Sour Dressing**

- 1/2 cup rice vinegar
- 2 1/3 Tbsp sugar
- 2 1/3 Tbsp soy sauce
- 1 tsp *shichimi togarashi* (seven spice mixture)

**1** Mince green onion and ginger; add to sauce ingredients and mix well.

**2** Cut chicken into bite-size pieces. Then flatten each piece by cutting as shown, so as to heat through quickly.

**3** Sprinkle chicken with salt and pepper.

**4** Dust chicken pieces with cornstarch, using a plastic bag as shown.

**5** Heat vegetable oil and deep-fry until crisp.

**6** Line a serving plate with lettuce strips, and place fried chicken. Pour over sweet and sour dressing.

Using knife at a slant, cut deeply into center towards right, and turn over knife opening meat towards right.

Put cornstarch and chicken in a plastic bag to dust evenly and also to keep your hands clean.

# BRAISED EGGPLANT

**Serves:** 4

6 Japanese-type eggplants
2 pods red hot pepper
1 tsp grated ginger root
1 cup *dashi* stock
4 1/2 Tbsp *mirin*
4 1/2 Tbsp soy sauce
*Kezuribushi* (Dried bonito
  shavings)
Vegetable oil for deep-frying

**1** Trim away caps from eggplants, and cut into half lengths. Score lengthwise as shown.

**2** Heat oil to 340°F (170°C) and deep-fry eggplant pieces until soft.

**3** In a saucepan, place *dashi*, *mirin*, soy sauce, red hot pepper and ginger juice, and heat to a boil. Add eggplants and bring to another boil. Turn off heat and let stand so eggplants absorb flavor well.

**4** Place in a serving bowl together with cooking sauce, and top with *kezuribushi*.

Score each piece so as to heat through quickly.

Deep-fry at 340°F (170°C) turning several times until heated through.

# *NATTO* DROP FRIES *(Natto no Kaki-age)*

**Serves:** 4

1 package (3 1/2 oz,100g)  *natto*
  (fermented soy beans)
3 1/2 oz (100 g) green peas
**Batter**
  ⌈ 1/2 beaten egg
  │ 100 ml water
  ⌊ 30 oz (60 g) flour
Vegetable oil for deep-frying
Pinch salt

**1** Combine batter ingredients.
**2** Add *natto* and green peas to batter. Mix only lightly so as not to let *natto* too sticky.
**3** Heat oil to 340°F (170°C). Spoon a small portion of *natto* mixture into hot oil and deep-fry, and flatten by unfolding center thickness with chopsticks.
**4** Serve with salt, in a small dish or sprinkled.

**Note**: When deep-frying, gently slide food from edge of oil. Do not panic when the mixture is scattered in oil. Put together and press down with a perforated spoon while batter has moisture. Turn over and press center to flatten.

**This type of *tempura* is called "*Kaki-age*", meaning gathered *tempura*.**

# FRIED FLOUNDER    The bony center turns into tasty crisps.

## Serves: 4

4 small flounder
Cornstarch for dusting
Vegetable oil for deep-frying
**Momiji-oroshi** (1/2 cup)
⌈4"(10 cm) length *daikon*
  radish
⌊1 pod red hot pepper
Scallions for condiment
*Ponzu* sauce

**1** Scrape off scales of flounder. Cut into center along backbone. Insert knife into the slit and work towards a side to separate flesh from bones as shown .
**2** Turn over and cut off flesh in the same manner. Save the bone with head and tail attached.
**3** Cut flesh into bite-size pieces. Dust with cornstarch. Dust bony portion as well.

**4** Heat oil to 340°F (170°C), and deep-fry bony portion at least 5 minutes. While frying, make *momiji-oroshi* : using a chopstick, thrust chili pepper into *daikon* and grate together.
**5** In 350°F (180°C) oil, deep-fry fish fillets until golden, few pieces at a time.

**6** On a serving plate, lay bony portion and place fried fish in a heap. Serve with shredded scallion, *momiji-oroshi*, and *ponzu* sauce.

### Separating flesh from bones

①**Make an incision along center, and insert tip of knife between flesh and bones.**

②**Separate the head side. Holding flesh with one hand, slide knife horizontally little by little.**

### Deep-frying bony portion

①**At first, lots of bubbles come up with sizzling sound.**

②When few bubbles appear on surface and the sound becomes lighter, it's ready to eat.

19

# CHILLED *TOFU* CHINESE STYLE *(Hiyayakko)*

## Jellyfish *Tofu*

**Serves: 4**
2 cakes *tofu*
3 ½ oz (100g) salted jellyfish
1 Japanese-type cucumber
**Sesame Dressing**
   3 Tbsp sesame paste
   1 tsp sugar
   2 Tbsp soy sauce
   Grated garlic

**1** Soak jellyfish in water until saltiness is removed. Change water several times.
**2** Blanch jellyfish in about 175°F (80°C) water. Crunchiness of jellyfish depends on this process. See photo to check the right temperature.
**3** Slice cucumbers thinly, and knead lightly with salt; squeeze out moisture.
**4** Cut *tofu* into quarters or dices.
**5** Combine dressing ingredients.

**6** In a serving dish, place *tofu* and top with cucumber slices and jellyfish. Pour over sesame dressing.

**Doneness of jellyfish depends on water temperature.**

The center example is crinkled right, whereas the left one is blanched at lower temperature, and the right at higher temperature.

## Duck Egg *Tofu*

**Serves: 4**
2 cakes *tofu*
1 preserved duck egg
1 knob ginger root
1/2 stalk green onion
3 1/2 oz (70 g) tienmen jang
           (hoisin sauce)
2/3 tsp kochu jang
           (Korean hot bean paste)

**1** Shell preserved duck egg and mince finely. Mince green onion and ginger root.
**2** Mix them with tienmen jang and kochu jang. Adjust amount of kochu jang to your taste.
**3** In a serving bowl, place cut *tofu* and pour over sauce.

**Note:** Combine sauce ingredients just before serving. As time goes, the moisture from green onion and ginger will thin the sauce.

Prepare sauce ingredients by mincing preserved duck egg, green onions and ginger root.

Since kochu jang is very hot, decrease amount if you prefer milder taste.

# YAM NOODLES *(Nagaimo Somen)*

### Serves: 4

1 lb (450 g) *nagaimo* (see p.14)
  Dash vinegar and salt
1/2 sheet *nori* seaweed
1/2 stalk green onion
*Mentsuyu* (*soba* soup base)
Dab of *wasabi*

**1** Peel *nagaimo* and sprinkle with vinegar to prevent discoloring.
**2** Using kitchen towel, wipe off jelly-like substance on surface of *nagaimo*. Cut into long, fine julienne strips.

**3** Sprinkle with salt sparingly. Let stand until supple.
**4** Mince green onion. Shred *nori*.
**5** In a serving bowl, lay salted *nagaimo* strips and garnish with shredded *nori* and green onion. Serve with *mentsuyu* and *wasabi*.

**Note**: Bottled *mentsuyu* or *sobatsuyu* is available in Japanese food section. Dilute as directed on the label.

By sprinkling with vinegar, *nagaimo* will stay white like real "*somen*".

Sprinkle with salt only lightly on one side. Too much salt will spoil the crispness.

# BELGIAN ENDIVE WITH *MENTAIKO*

### Serves: 4

2 heads  Belgian endive
3 oz (90 g)  butter
2 oz (60 g)  *mentaiko*
         (chili cod roe)

**1** Soften butter at room temperature.
**2** Remove skin of *mentaiko* as shown below.
**3** Mix butter and *mentaiko*.
**4** Using back of a spoon, spread *mentaiko* butter inside each leaf as shown.

**Note**: Spread thinly so you can enjoy the taste of both the paste and endive. *Mentaiko* butter can be enjoyed spread over thin slices of French bread or mixed in potato salads.

Cut skin lengthwise and open to sides. Using back of knife, scrape off inside.

*Mentaiko* butter can be easily spread over the inside of leaves using back of a spoon.

# SAUTEED CALAMARI WITH *ENOKIDAKE*

## This is a richer tasting version with delicate mushrooms preferred with drinks or rice.

**Serves:** 4

4 calamari, about ²/₃ lb (300 g)
2 packages *enokidake* mushrooms
1/2 clove garlic, minced
1 Tbsp vegetable oil
2 Tbsp butter
1/3 tsp salt
2 tsp soy sauce

**1** Cut off root ends of *enokidake* mushrooms as shown; discard.
**2** Splitting into segments, remove sawdust between ends. (Natural sawdust is used for cultivation of *enokidake*, packed in glass jars.)
**3** Remove inside of calamari, including transparent cartilage. Rinse and cut into bite-size pieces. Cut up tentacles as well. Parboil 2 minutes and drain. Set aside.

**4** In a skillet, heat vegetable oil and butter. Fry minced garlic until the aroma is released. Remove from heat. When the skillet is a bit cooled, add calamari and mushrooms and stir-fry just until mushrooms are supple over medium-low heat (High heat may make calamari tough.) Season with salt and soy sauce.

**Note**: Because calamari are so tasty, they are served in many different ways in Japan; *sashimi* when fresh, *sunomono* (vine-gared dish), *nimono* (simmered dish), *shiokara* (salted preserve) and so on. Do not overcook calamari as it may cause toughness to chew.

Discard bases of mushrooms at about 1/2 " (1.5 cm) from ends .

Break up and remove sawdust near ends.

# *KONNYAKU* AND *SHIMEJI*

**Serves:** 4

1 *konnyaku* (yam cake)
1 package *shimeji* mushrooms
1 cup *dashi* stock
4 Tbsp *mirin*
3 Tbsp light soy sauce
3 *umeboshi* (pickled Japanese plums)
*Kezuribushi* (dried bonito shavings)

**1** Remove stones from *ume-boshi*. Mince flesh until smooth as shown below.
**2** Slice *konnyaku* into thin

squares and cook in boiling water 1-2 minutes.
**3** Separate *shimeji* mushrooms into segments.
**4** In a saucepan, bring *dashi*, *mirin* and light soy sauce to a boil. Add *konnyaku* and mushrooms and cook about 10 minutes or until the flavor is absorbed.
**5** Drain in a colander. In a bowl, mix them with *umeboshi* paste until evenly coated.
**6** Serve sprinkled with *kezuri-bushi*.

Mince *umeboshi* flesh as finely as possible.

Parboiling *konnyaku* is essential to remove odor.

# SIMMERED *SHIRATAKI*

### Serves: 4

1 package *shirataki*
    (yam noodles)
3 1/2 oz (100 g) fresh or salted
    cod roe (*tarako*)
2 oz (60g) carrot
*Mitsuba* (trefoil), optional

**Cooking Sauce**
> 1/4 cup *dashi* stock
> 4 Tbsp *mirin*
> 3 Tbsp light soy sauce

**1** Parboil *shirataki* in ample water. Drain and cut up.
**2** Split cod roe into halves, then cut into 3/8" (1 cm) slices.
**3** Shred carrot finely. Cut *mitsuba* stalks into the same lengths.
**4** In a saucepan, bring sauce ingredients to a boil. Add *shirataki*. Add cod roe, constantly crumbling with chopsticks or fork.
**5** Add carrot and cook briefly until the flavor is absorbed. Add *mitsuba* and immediately remove from heat.
**6** Place in a serving bowl in a around.

**Note 1**: Salted cod roe may be substituted with fresh one. In this case, decrease soy sauce to 1 Tbsp.
**Note 2**: This flavorful yet low calorie dish is called "*masago-ni*", meaning simmered food with white sand. Ground chicken or pork can make a good substitute for cod roe.

**Crumble cod roe quickly so as not to avoid hard lumps.**

# FISH CAKE WITH RADISH

### Serves: 4

1 small *kamaboko*
    (steamed fish cake)
6 *myoga* sprouts
1 cup grated *daikon* radish
2 Tbsp sugar
3 Tbsp rice vinegar
1 Tbsp or less light soy sauce

**1** Split *myoga* sprouts and slice thinly. Cut *kamaboko* into julienne strips.
**2** Combine sugar, rice vinegar and light soy sauce and stir in grated *daikon* radish.
**3** Just before serving, mix everything and place in individual serving bowls.

**Note 1**: Substitute *myoga* with celery.
**Note 2**: This type of dish is called "*ae-mono*", and for the best result, mix with sauce or dressing just before serving. Crispness of *myoga* will be spoiled if mixed ahead of time.

**1**

**Prepare ingredients. Blanch *myoga* slices in cold water.**

**2**

Blend seasonings and add to grated *daikon* radish. Just mix everything and serve immediately.

# SPICY CUCUMBERS

## Serves: 4

2 Japanese-type cucumbers
2 fillets chicken
2 Tbsp toban jang
    (hot bean paste)
1/3 tsp salt
1 Tbsp sesame oil

**1** Crack whole cucumbers by pounding with your fist as shown.

**2** Twist cucumbers and break into bite-size pieces as shown left.

**3** Boil chicken and plunge into cold water; drain and pat dry. Slice chicken as shown.

**4** Mix with seasonings in order: first coat with sesame oil, then sprinkle with salt. Stir in hot bean paste. Serve chilled.

**Note**: Adjust boiling time according to your taste. Cook thoroughly unless using very fresh chicken.

**1** Pounding with your fist several times, crack cucumbers on a chopping board.

**2** Break into pieces by twisting with your hands.

**3** Slice chicken using knife at a slant.

---

**Note:** Pink peppercorn is the same species as common black pepper, but is harvested before maturity.

# LEMON TURNIPS (*Kabu Lemon-zuke*)

## Serves: 4

6 Japanese turnips with greens
 1 heap Tbsp salt
1 lemon
2 Tbsp pink peppercorn
2 Tbsp salt
1 Tbsp sugar
3 Tbsp vegetable oil

**1** Cut turnips into halves or quarters, then slice into 1/8" (3 mm) thicknesses. Blanch turnip greens in boiling water and plunge into cold water; cut up.

**2** In a bowl dissolve salt in 2 cups of water. Soak turnip slices and let stand until supple; drain and squeeze out moisture.

**3** Peel lemon. Shred peel and blanch in boiling water; drain. This way chemicals on surface can be removed.

**4** Trim away pulp from lemon and cut into thin half-moon slices.

**5** Combine salt, sugar and oil. Mix all ingredients and toss well.

**1** Blanching turnip greens makes the taste milder. Be sure to cool immediately to retain color and texture.

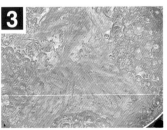

**3** Also blanch lemon peels in boiling water so as to soften the fragrance (and sterilize surface).

# MUSTARD EGGPLANT

## Serves: 4

5 Japanese-type eggplants
- 1 cup water
- 2 Tbsp salt

**Marinade**
- 2 Tbsp hot mustard paste
- 1 Tbsp sugar
- 2 Tbsp soy sauce

*Kezuribushi* (dried bonito shavings)

**1** Dissolve salt in water in a bowl. Cut eggplant into half lengths, then slice each thinly lengthwise; soak in lightly salted water to retain color.

**2** Combine marinade ingredients.

**3** When eggplant slices are supple, drain and pour over marinade. Mix well and chill at least 30 minutes. Serve sprinkled with *kezuribushi*.

Cut edges of eggplant may turn brown quickly. Repeat slice-and-drop procedure.

# LAYERED CABBAGE SALAD

## Serves: 4

5 oz (150 g) *hidara* (dried codfish), or smoked salmon
6 cabbage leaves
10 *shiso* (perilla) leaves
4" (10 cm) length carrot
Lightly salted water

**1** Trim away hard stem bases of cabbage leaves. Soak in salted water together with dried codfish; let stand overnight or until cabbage leaves are supple and codfish releases extra saltiness. Save salty water.

**2** Remove bones from codfish as shown, and cut into 1/4" (6 mm) widths. If using smoked salmon, just slice thinly.

**3** Shred carrot and mix lightly with codfish pieces.

**4** Line a baking dish with plastic wrap so you can take out without turning over.

**5** Lay cabbage leaf, *shiso* leaves, then carrot and codfish. Repeat this until all ingredients are layered. Pour over reserved salty water. Place another baking dish filled with water as a weight, and marinate for 30 minutes.

Debone carefully, as bones of dried cod are hard and clinging to flesh.

Make layers of vegetables and fish evenly. Cover with a plastic wrap, and place a weight.

# SEA BREAM WITH MUSTARD SAUCE

## Serves: 4

5 oz (150 g) sea bream or red snapper fillet for *sashimi*
1 Japanese-type cucumber
2" (5 cm) length *daikon* radish
1/2 red onion

**Mustard Sauce**
- 1/4 cup rice vinegar
- 2 tsp sugar
- 3 Tbsp light soy sauce
- 2 Tbsp whole grain mustard
- 4 Tbsp vegetable oil

**1** Shred *daikon*, cucumber and red onion; soak in cold water until crisp.
**2** Make 2 lengthwise incisions on skin side of fish fillet as shown.
**3** Pour boiling water over fillet.
**4** Plunge into ice water to prevent cooking; drain and slice very thinly.
**5** Combine sauce ingredients.
**6** In a serving plate, lay well-drained vegetables, and place fish slices.
**7** Pour over mustard sauce just before serving.

**Note:** Use this sauce to enhance other white meat *sashimi*.

Make 2 lengthwise incisions on skin side of fish fillet.

Pour boiling water over fillet.

Plunge into ice water to prevent cooking.

# ASPARAGUS AND GARLIC *TEMPURA*

**1** Prepare asparagus. Peel tough ends and cut into 1 1/2"(4 cm) lengths.
**2** Remove skin of garlic cloves as shown below.
**3** Combine batter ingredients.
**4** Dip in *tempura* batter and deep-fry until crisp. Sprinkle with Spicy Salt and serve.

**Note**: When using lots of garlic cloves, use the method below. This will also work when peeling outer skin of onions.

### How to remove garlic skin

If peeling several cloves, soak in water for a while. This will help you peel skin easily.

### How to soften garlic smell

For those who like taste of garlic but not the smell, dry in a basket for a day, in a shade.

## Serves: 4

5 oz (150 g) fresh asparagus
2 garlic bulbs
Vegetable oil for deep-frying

*Tempura* **Batter**
- 1 egg yolk
- 100 ml water
- 2 oz (60 g) cake flour

Crazy Salt

# CRAB AND *SHIMEJI* GRATIN
## (*Kani to Shimeji no Uni-yaki*)

### Serves: 4

4 oz (120 g) crabmeat
1 package *shimeji* mushrooms
**Tamago no Moto**

1 egg
200 ml vegetable oil
1 tsp salt

2 Tbsp bottled sea urchin paste
(*neri-uni*)
2 Tbsp butter

**1** Make *tamago no moto*, as illustrated below. To stabilize mixing bowl, lay a wet cloth underneath. Add a small amount of oil and start whipping at edge, tilting the bowl.
**2** Add sea urchin paste and stir as illustrated right.
**3** Separate *shimeji* mushrooms. In an ovenproof serving bowl, arrange mushrooms and crabmeat. Pour *Tamago no moto* and top with a piece of butter. In a preheated 400°F (200°C) oven, cook 10

minutes until surface is browned.

**Tamago no moto** : Oil helps food taste milder and richer, as you know with salad dressings enriched by oil. However, if oil is mixed on its own, the sauce will separate. Eggs not only prevent this separation, but work as an emulsifier. This sauce is called "*Tamago no moto*" and is prized for its fluffy texture and richer flavor.

Add sea urchin paste to *tamago no moto* and stir. Use this sauce for grilling fish or vegetables.

## How to make *Tamago no moto*

① Stir egg yolk and gradually add vegetable oil, beginning with 1 tsp. Do not add a large amount at a time.
② Drizzle in remaining oil, whipping constantly. Blend in salt.
③ When the mixture sticks to whisk, add egg white and whip until well blended.

# COD MILT WITH HORSERADISH SAUCE
## (*Shirako no Wasabi* Sauce)

### Serves: 4

7 oz(200 g) cod milt
 Flour for dusting
Dash vegetable oil
1 small tomato
1/2 Japanese-type cucumber
**Horseradish Sauce**

2/3 cup grated *daikon* radish
2 Tbsp ketchup
1 Tbsp *wasabi* paste
1 Tbsp soy sauce
2 Tbsp lemon juice
2 Tbsp white wine

**1** Drain grated *daikon* in a colander.
**2** Cut tomato into small cubes. Cut cucumber into thick quarter-moons.
**3** Combine sauce ingredients and marinate cucumber and

tomato pieces.
**4** Cut up milt and dust with flour. In a skillet, heat small amount of oil and fry milt until both sides are slightly browned.
**5** In a serving dish, arrange milt in a heap, and pour over sauce.

Grated *daikon* should be drained well since extra moisture will thin the sauce.

# BOILED RADISH IN THICK SAUCE
## (Furofuki Daikon Kani-an)

### Serves: 4

6" (15cm) length *daikon* radish
4 oz (120g) crabmeat
3 stalks scallions

**Thick Sauce**

1 2/3 cups *dashi* stock
3 Tbsp Chinese wine
2 Tbsp oyster sauce
1 tsp salt
1 Tbsp cornstarch, dissolved in same amount of water

**1** Use only middle of *daikon* radish, about 6" (15cm) in length (see below). Cut into 1 1/8"-1 1/2" (3-4cm) rounds and peel.

**2** Trim away one side of each *daikon* piece. Turn over and make a crisscross incision so seasonings will penetrate quickly and evenly.

**3** In a saucepan cook *daikon* in water to cover, until soft.

**4** In a small saucepan heat sauce ingredients to a boil. Add crabmeat and cut up scallions; remove from heat immediately.

**5** Place *daikon* in a serving bowl, and pour over thick sauce.

### How to peel *daikon*

Slice into rounds before peeling the skin, for a smooth surface (right).

For simmered dish, middle part is most suitable as it is tender and also retain shape.

Make "secret" incision into each bottom of *daikon* round. It helps with absorbing flavor fast.

# FISH WITH SOUR PLUM DRESSING

### Serves: 4

1/2 lb (230 g) fish fillets
Cornstarch for dusting
1 package *daikon* sprouts
1 small head Belgium endive
2 oz ( 60 g) snow peas, cooked

**Sour Plum Sauce**

1 1/3 oz(40 g) *umeboshi* (pickled Japanese plum)
2 tsp sugar
4 Tbsp water
1 Tbsp sugar
3 Tbsp vegetable oil

**1** Cut fish fillets into bite-size pieces and sprinkle with salt. Dust with cornstarch.

**2** In boiling water, cook fish pieces and plunge into ice water to stop cooking; drain.

**3** Trim away root ends of *daikon* sprouts. Cut Belgium endive and boiled snow peas diagonally; soak in cold water and set aside.

**4** Make dressing. Mince *umeboshi* finely to make a paste. Mix this paste with sugar, water and vegetable oil until well blended.

**5** On a serving dish, heap drained vegetables in center. Arrange fish pieces around them and pour plum dressing as shown.

**Note:** Try this refreshing salad with white meat fish such as yellowtail, bass, or sword fish.

Do not overcook fish as it spoils texture. Prepare ice water before cooking fish pieces.

# STEAMED *TOFU* DUMPLING

**Serves: 4**

3 1/2 oz (100g) fish fillets
1 cake firm *tofu*
1 egg, beaten
1/2 tsp salt

**Thick Sauce**

- 1 2/3 cups *dashi* stock
- 1/4 cup *mirin*
- 1/4 cup soy sauce
- 1 Tbsp cornstarch, dissolved in same amount of water

**Condiments**

- Shredded green onion
- Grated ginger root

**1** Cut fish fillets into 3/8" (1cm) cubes.

**2** Strain *tofu*, by thrusting through a sieve or strainer.

**3** Add beaten egg to *tofu* and stir well until well blended. Stir in salt, then fish pieces.

**4** Line a small dish with a plastic wrap. Place a quarter portion of *tofu* mixture in center, and shape into a ball, letting air out. See left for shaping.

**5** In a preheated steamer, steam wrapped *tofu* mixture 20 minutes over low heat.

**6** In a small saucepan, heat *dashi* stock, *mirin* and soy sauce to a boil. Remove from heat and stir in dissolved cornstarch. Heat through, stirring constantly.

**7** Place a steamed dumpling in individual serving bowl, and pour over thick sauce. Garnish with sliced green onion and grated ginger in a heap.

**Note**: Use a heatproof plastic wrap that do not release plastic odor.

**4**
① **Bring opposite corners of plastic wrap. Bring up one side corner and make even pleats pulling upward.**
② **Bring up remaining corner, pleating evenly as well. Be sure to let air out, and bind top with elastic.**

**2**
**Straining *tofu* is an essential process to create an extra smoothness.**

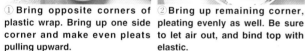

# FRIED EGGPLANT IN THICK SAUCE

**Serves: 4**

4 Japanese-type eggplants
  Vegetable oil for deep-frying
7 oz (200g) cooked *anago* (conger eel), or fish fillets
6 *shiso* (perilla) leaves

**Thick Sauce**

- 1 2/3 cups *dashi* stock
- 1/2 cup *mirin*
- 1/2 cup soy sauce
- 2 Tbsp cornstarch, dissolved in same amount of water

**1** Grill eel to brown both surfaces. Cut into 1/4" (6mm) widths.

**2** Cut eggplants into quarters, and make a few incisions diagonally over skin.

**3** Heat oil to 340°F(170°C), and deep-fry eggplant pieces until surfaces are soft when pushed; drain.

**4** In a small saucepan heat *dashi* stock, *mirin* and soy sauce to a boil. Remove from heat and stir in dissolved cornstarch. Add eel and heat through, stirring constantly.

**5** Shred *shiso* leaves.

**6** Arrange drained eggplants in a serving dish and pour over thick sauce. Garnish with shredded *shiso* leaves.

**Note**: Try with other white meat fish that is firm in texture. Ground chicken or pork also makes a good sauce.

# SAVORY EGG CUSTARD *(Hiyashi Chawan-mushi)*

## Serves: 4

2 eggs

(A)
- 200 ml *dashi* stock
- 200 ml milk
- 1 tsp salt
- 2 Tbsp *sake*
- 1 tsp light soy sauce

3 *shiitake* mushrooms
1 1/2" (4cm) length carrot
1 medium potato
2 Tbsp butter
1 Tbsp vegetable oil
Salt and pepper

**Clear Soup**
- 200 ml water
- 1 chicken bouillon
- 2 tsp light soy sauce

**1** Peel and cut carrot and potato into 3/8" (1 cm) cubes as shown. Cut *shiitake* into same size cubes.

**2** In a skillet, heat butter and vegetable oil. Add vegetables, stir-fry briefly and season with salt and pepper. To retain resilience, do not cook completely at this point since they are to be steamed later.

**3** Beat eggs using a fork until you get uniform consistency. Blend in seasonings **(A)**.

**4** In individual serving cups, pour 2/3 amount of egg mixture. Steam over low heat as shown right.

**5** When egg is almost set, add vegetables and pour in remaining egg mixture. Steam again until set. This way, vegetable pieces are visible as they do not sink.

**6** Bring sauce ingredients to a boil and remove from heat; set aside.

**7** Chill steamed custard cups in refrigerator. Pour in clear soup. Do not chill soup, as it becomes opaque. Serve while the sauce is lukewarm.

## Hint for steaming

**Cover steamer with oversized kitchen cloth to avoid dripping inside. Put lid, sliding a little. This way you can avoid bubbly texture.**

**Prepare vegetables by cutting into same sized cubes.**

**Stir-fry only briefly and do not brown. Remove from heat before they are completely cooked.**

**Add vegetables when 2/3 of egg mixture is almost set. Pour in remaining mixture.**

30

# ONSEN-BOILED EGG
## *(Onsen Tamago)*

**Serves:** 4

4 eggs
**Tomato Sauce**
 1 small tomato
 2 Tbsp minced onion
 1 stalk scallion
 1/3 cup rice vinegar
 1 Tbsp sugar
 2 Tbsp light soy sauce
 Dash black pepper

**Always check the temperature**

Temperature control is essential to make *onsen*-boiled eggs. Maintain 150°F (65°C).

**1** In a stainless pot, heat water to 120°F (50°C) and add eggs. Reheat slowly to 150°F (65°C), and turn off heat. Let stand 30-40 minutes, covered. If temperature gets lower, heat again to maintain 150°F (65°C). Drain and chill.

**2** Make sauce. Dip tomato in boiling water and peel skin. Remove seeds and mince finely. Combine with other sauce ingredients and chill.

**3** Into each individual serving bowl, break an egg and add tomato sauce.

**Note:** Originally, *onsen*-egg is boiled in natural hot spring water, which cooks only the yolk and the white remains smooth like jelly. Be careful to keep the temperature since the egg white will also set when it raises as high as 158°F (70°C).

# CHICKEN MOLD

**Serves:** 4

1 lb (450g) chicken thigh
6 cups water
1 cup *sake*
1 1/2 tsp salt
 1 Tbsp unflavored gelatin
 4 Tbsp water
1/2 Japanese-type cucumber
1 egg, beaten
Shredded scallion
*Momiji-oroshi* (see p.19)
*Ponzu* (citrus vinegar)

**1** Trim away skin and fat from chicken; cut up.

**2** In a saucepan put water and chicken. Bring to a boil and remoce scum. Add *sake* and simmer over low heat for 2 hours. Sprinkle gelatin over measured water; let stand 15 minutes. Add this and salt to saucepan; remove from heat.

**3** Shred cucumber and soak in lightly salted water until supple; squeeze out water.

**4** Make thin omelets. Beat egg with pinch of salt and pour 1/3 amount into a non-stick skillet and cook until set. Repeat with remaining egg and shred thinly.

**5** When the saucepan is lukewarm, stir in cucumber and shredded omelet. Pour into molds and chill.

Remove skin and fat from chicken. Skin is added to cooking liquid to extract gelatin.

Simmer chicken 2 hours until liquid reduces to 1/3.

# ASPARAGUS ON JELLY

**Serves: 4**
6 spears fresh asparagus
1 3/4 oz (50g) *kuzukiri*
1 small carrot, grated
1/2 small onion, grated
**Dressing**
- 1/3 cup rice vinegar
- 1 Tbsp sugar
- 2 Tbsp light soy sauce
- 1/4 cup vegetable oil

**1** Peel tough ends of asparagus and cut into 3, as shown below.
**2** Cook in salted, boiling water, and plunge into cold water to retain color.
**3** Cook *kuzukiri* in ample boiling water 5 minutes, constantly stirring so they do not stick each other. Turn off heat and let steam, covered for 10-15 minutes. Drain and chill soaked in cold water.
**4** Combine dressing ingredients and stir in grated carrot and onion.
**5** In a serving dish, place drained *kuzukiri* and asparagus. Pour over dressing.

Do not discard hard ends. Just peel skin.

Cook hard ends first for 30 seconds, then add remainder to cook evenly.

# PUNGENT AVOCADO SALAD

**Serves: 4**
4 oz (120g) shrimp, deveined
1 ripe avocado
2 tsp *wasabi* paste
4 tsp mayonnaise
1 Tbsp soy sauce

**1** Shell shrimp and cook in boiling water briefly; plunge into cold water and drain immediately. Cut into 1" (2.5cm) lengths.
**2** Cut avocado into halves and remove pit. Peel and cut into cubes or the same size as shrimp.
**3** Mix mayonnaise, *wasabi* and soy sauce and stir until well blended; toss with avocado and shrimp.

**Note:** *Wasabi* and soy sauce make the difference. Adjust the amount of *wasabi* to your taste.

### Use ripened avocado
Green avocados with black spots at left are not ripened enough to eat as a salad. Wait until the skin turns black.

# MARINATED HORSE MACKEREL IN HOT SAUCE

**Serves: 4**

20 tiny horse mackerel
   Flour for dusting
   Vegetable oil for deep-frying
1 bundle yellow garlic chives
1 knob ginger root
2 pods red hot peppers
1/2 cup vinegar
3 Tbsp sugar
2 Tbsp soy sauce
Some Iceberg lettuce leaves

**1** Prepare horse mackerel. Push up gills as shown with your fingers.
**2** Hold base of gills and pull out inside as shown.
**3** Wipe with wet towel. Do not rinse in water as fish will become too wet. Dust each fish with flour.
**4** In 340°F(170°C) oil, deep-fry horse mackerel 15-10 minutes.
**5** Cut yellow garlic chives into 1"(2.5cm) lengths. Mince gingerroot. Seed red peppers and slice thinly.
**6** Mix vinegar, sugar and soy sauce, add ginger root and red pepper. Mix in yellow garlic chives.
**7** In a serving dish, lay fried horse mackerel and pour over sauce.

**Note 1:** Deep-fry whole fish long enough until tails and small bones are crisp and edible. Fry over low heat. At first, lots of bubbles come up with sizzling sound. When ready, few bubbles appear on surface and the sound becomes lighter. Drain oil.

**Note 2:** To enjoy the crispness of fried fish, do not marinate and just pour over the dressing.

**1**

First, open gills with one hand so the base part can be easily held with the other hand.

**2**

Pull off the base part, and voila! The inside is pulled out easily.

**3**

Inside can be removed in one motion as long as fish is very fresh. Do not rinse.

**7**

Pour over dressing while fish is hot so it absorbs flavor fast.

33

# CHICKEN CRISPS

**Serves:** 4
2 chicken fillets
Cornstarch for dusting
1 egg white, beaten
White sesame seed
Pinch salt

**1** prepare chicken fillets as shown above right. Turn over meat and pull them apart with your hand and back of knife.
**2** Sandwich fillets between plastic wrap, leaving some room to spread. Using a wine bottle or flat side of a meat mallet, pound meat as shown until paper thin, into about 1/24"(1mm) thickness.
**3** Remove upper wrap, and sprinkle chicken with cornstarch only lightly. Brush on egg white, and coat with sesame seed. Cut into bite size pieces.
**4** In 340°F(170°C) oil, deep-fry until golden. Sprinkle with salt.

**1**

**Make scores among sides of tendon before pulling it off using back of knife.**

**2**

**Bad example**

**Pound carefully so meat spread evenly. Do not pound one spot as it may cause breakage.**

# BRAISED SOY BEANS AND PORK

**Serves:** 4
3 1/2 oz (100g) soy beans
1/3 lb (150 g) boneless pork rib
1 cup *dashi* stock
1/3 cup sugar
1/3 cup soy sauce
Vegetable oil for deep-frying

**1** Soak dried soy beans in water overnight.
**2** Cut pork into 3/4"(2cm) cubes.
**3** In 360°F(180°C) oil, deep-fry soy beans and pork separately until lightly browned; drain.
**4** Bring ample water to a boil and add soy beans and pork. Drain immediately as shown. This way extra oil is removed and also seasoning will penetrate fast.
**5** In a saucepan, place drained beans and pork. Add *dashi* stock, sugar, soy sauce and water to cover. Simmer over

low heat about 1 hour but not longer.

**Note 1:** When deep-frying soy beans, use a large wok or pan, since oil may bubble and spill out. This can be also avoided by using small amount of oil.
**Note 2:** Blanching in hot oil shortens cooking time. This dish is delicious hot or cold.

**4**

**Wash off extra oil by blanching in hot water.**

# CELERY LEAVES WITH GINGER

**Serves: 2**

1 stalk celery (use only leaves)
2 knobs(3 oz/90g) fresh ginger root
1 Tbsp or less vegetable oil
2 Tbsp *sake*
1 Tbsp soy sauce

**1** In ample boiling water, cook celery leaves briefly; drain and mince.

**2** Shred ginger root finely and soak in water for 5-10 minutes; drain.

**3** Heat oil in a skillet, and stir-fry celery leaves and ginger root slivers. Season with *sake* and soy sauce. Serve individually in small bowls.

**Note:** Pungency and crispness of fresh ginger root are the key. Ginger root contains lots of carbohydrate which tends to scorch easily. By soaking cut ginger root, scorching can be avoided.

Prevent ginger root from scorching by soaking in water.

Add drained ginger root to celery and stir-fry briefly over high heat.

# FRIED *TAKUAN* PICKLE

**Serves: 4**

5 oz (150g) aged *takuan* (pickled *daikon* radish)
2 pods red hot peppers
2 Tbsp vegetable oil
3 Tbsp *sake*
2 Tbsp soy sauce
White sesame seed

**1** If using aged *takuan*, soak in water as shown below, to remove saltiness. Check saltiness after a while. Soak until it does taste salty.

**2** Slice thinly.

**3** Heat oil in a skillet, add red peppers, then stir-fry *takuan* slices with *sake* and soy sauce.

**4** Place in individual serving bowls, sprinkled with toasted sesame seed.

**Note:** This is a good way of utilizing aged *takuan* that is turning somewhat sour. Fresh *takuan* can be used of course. Try with pickled *Takana* (Chinese mustard green.)

**Preparation**

Remove saltiness of pickled radish by soaking in water for a while.

# BEEF TENDON AND *DAIKON*

## Serves: 4

1/3 lb(300g) beef tendon
1/2 *daikon* radish, peeled
1 small knob ginger root
1/2 cup *sake*
1/3 cup sugar
1/2 cup *mirin*
1/2 cup soy sauce
Green onion
Ginger root skin
1 bulb garlic, skinned

**1** Trim away fat from beef tendon (see below), and cut up.
**2** Bring ample water to a boil and add beef tendon pieces. Bring to another boil and discard water. This way extra fat and odor are removed.
**3** Cook beef tendon, *sake*, green onion, and ginger in ample water. Remore scum. Cover and cook over low heat 1 hour.
**4** When liquid is reduced to half, add cut-up *daikon* and remaining seasonings. Cook another hour.
**5** Add garlic cloves 10 minutes before serving. Garnish with shredded ginger root.

Too much fat spoils flavor. Trim away excess before cooking.

Meat odor will be removed by adding green onion and ginger root skin to water.

# CELERY AND CHICKEN SALAD

## Serves: 4

4 oz (120g) chicken breast
  80 ml water
  2 Tbsp *sake*
  1/2 tsp salt
1 stalk celery
1 Japanese-type cucumber
1/2 red onion
1/2 baby broccoli

**Tangy Dressing**
  2 tsp ginger juice
  1/3 cup rice vinegar
  2 Tbsp soy sauce
  2 tsp sugar
  1 Tbsp sesame oil
  1 Tbsp vegetable oil

**1** Trim celery stalk and remove coarse strings. Cut into 2"(5cm) lengths and then into thin slices. Soak in ice water.
**2** Combine water, *sake* and salt in a saucepan. Bring to a boil and add chicken. Cover and cook until well cooked; let stand to cool.
**3** Split cucumbers lengthwise, and slice into same size as celery. Slice red onion and soak in water until crisp.
**4** Prepare baby broccoli: cut incisions into tough ends, then cut each into 3. Cook in boiling water, beginning with tough ends; squeeze out moisture.
**5** Mix drained vegetables and chicken and place in a serving dish. Combine dressing ingredients and pour over salad.

Cut baby broccoli into 3 and cook, base part first, followed by middle part.

# FISH AND GARLIC CROQUETTES

**Makes: 8**

4 medium potatoes
1/3 lb (150g) lightly salted cod fillets
1 bulb garlic
Salt and pepper
Flour, for dusting
l egg, beaten
Breadcrumbs
Vegetable oil for deep-frying

**Tartar Sauce**
- 1/3 cup mayonnaise
- 1 hard-boiled egg
- 1 Tbsp minced parsley
- 2 Tbsp minced onion

Lemon wedges
Shredded cabbage

**1** Peel garlic. To save time, soak unpeeled garlic cloves in water for a while as shown.

**2** To soften garlic odor, microwave 2 minutes as shown.

**3** Boil or microwave potatoes. While warm, skin and mash roughly using a pestle or potato masher.

**4** Cut salted cod into 1" (2.5cm) pieces. Mix mashed potatoes with cod, garlic, salt and pepper.

**5** Divide into 8 portions. Form into 8 oblong balls.

**6** Dust with flour, dip in beaten egg, and coat with breadcrumbs. Deep-fry until golden.

**7** Combine tartar sauce ingredients.

**8** Soak shredded cabbage in water until crisp, and drain.

**9** In a serving dish, arrange cabbage and croquettes. Garnish with tartar sauce and lemon wedge.

When peeling many cloves, soak in water to soften skin for easy removing.

Wrap peeled garlic cloves in a plastic wrap and microwave, to reduce strong odor.

Mash potatoes roughly so they do not produce gluten.

Divide mixture into portions before shaping into balls.

37

# MARINATED SABLEFISH
## (Gintara Saikyo-zuke)

**Serves: 4**
4 sablefish fillets
**Marinade**
- 4 oz (120g) *saikyo miso* (sweet bean paste)
- 2 Tbsp *sake*

**1** Make marinade. Thin *miso* paste with *sake* as shown below.

**2** Use a whisk for smooth blending.

**3** In an air-tight container, place half *miso* mixture. Lay sablefish fillets and cover with remaining *miso* mixture. Refrigerate overnight.

**4** Scrape off marinade, and quickly rinse in water; dry with a towel.

**5** Over direct flame or in a preheated grill, cook fish fillets until browned.

### *Saikyo miso* and white *miso*
*Saikyo miso* and common white *miso* resemble in appearance. *Saikyo miso* (right) has finer and stickier texture and is less salty than white *miso*.

Add *sake*, a little portion at a time, to *saikyo miso*.

Using a whisk, stir until a peak is formed when whisk is lifted.

# STEWED BEEF JAPANESE STYLE

**Serves: 4**
1 lb (450g) beef for stew
8 taro yams
1 *konnyaku* (yam cake)
8 pods snowpea, cooked
1 knob ginger root
3 Tbsp sugar
1/3 cup *mirin*
1/3 cup soy sauce
1 2/3 oz (50g) *saikyo miso*
3 Tbsp fresh cream

**1** Cut up beef and cook in covering water 1 hour. Add green onion and ginger skin if in hand, to enhance fragrance.

**2** Cook peeled taros in boiling water. Parboil sliced *konnyaku*.

**3** When cooking liquid reduces below surfaces of meat, add sugar, *mirin*, and soy sauce. Also add parboiled taros and *konnyaku*, and cook 30 minutes.

**4** Stir in *saikyo miso* and continue to simmer another 30 minutes.

**5** Add cream for a richer flavor. Garnish with shredded ginger root and snowpeas.

Parboil vegetables before adding to pot.

Stir in fresh cream just before turning off heat.

# SHRIMP MIX *TEMPURA* (*Ebi Kaki-age*)

**Serves: 4**

¼ lb (120g) fresh asparagus
5 oz (150g) shrimp, shelled
   and deveined
***Tempura* Batter**

⎰ 1 egg yolk
⎱ 200 ml water
⎱ 3/4 cup cake flour

Salt
4 lemon wedges

**1** Peel tough ends of asparagus, and cut diagonally into 1" (2.5cm) slices.
**2** In a bowl, combine batter ingredients. Fold lightly, but do not stir.
**3** Add shrimp and asparagus to batter and mix lightly. Spoon a little portion gently side into heated oil.
**4** To achieve a fluffy, crisp *tempura*, see illustrations below.

**Note:** If *tempura* has openings, pressing is not necessary. Remove scattered batter occasionally.

### Drain oil when crisp and golden.

The key to such dry and crisp *tempura* is to maintain oil temperature(340°F-350°F/170°C-180°C). Fry a small batch at a time. Also, do not heat up too long as batter turns brown before the inside is cooked.

① Slide in from the edge of oil, and spread with chopsticks to flatten.

② Shape into a round, holding edges with a strainer.

③ While still soft, turn over and pierce center so as to heat through evenly.

# FLUFFY FISH POT

**Serves: 4**

1/2 lb (230g) fish fillet
1/2 lb (230g) spring starflower
   or garlic chives
200 ml milk
3 Tbsp right soy sauce
2 eggs, beaten
1 3/4 oz (50g) natural cheese

**1** Use only tender part of garlic chives for this fluffy and savory custard. Cut into 1"(2.5cm) lengths.
**2** Cut fish fillet into 1"(2.5cm) pieces. Blanch in boiling water; drain.
**3** In fireproof, individual serving dishes, pour in milk and soy sauce. Add garlic chives and bring to a boil over low heat.
**4** Add fish pieces, drizzle in beaten eggs. Top with sliced natural cheese. When eggs are almost set, remove from heat. Serve while hot.

If using spring starflower, tear off tough ends and use only tender part.

After pouring in egg, do not overcook so as to achieve a fluffy texture.

# ROCKFISH WITH BALSAMIC SAUCE

**Serves:** 4

2 darkbanded rockfish
  Flour for dusting
  Vegetable oil for frying
1 package *shimeji* mushrooms
3 red-leaf lettuce
**Balsamic Sauce**
  4 Tbsp balsamic vinegar
  2 Tbsp soy sauce
  3 Tbsp butter
Chives

**1** Cut rockfish into fillets. Cut into bite-size pieces and dust lightly with flour.
**2** Heat some oil in a skillet, and fry fish pieces, skin side first. When edges turn whitish, turn over and cook.
**3** Separate *shimeji* mushrooms into segments, and stir-fry in hot oil.
**4** Make balsamic sauce. In a small saucepan, place sauce ingredients and cook over low heat until thickened .
**5** On a serving plate, place red leaf lettuce leaves and mushrooms. Place fish pieces on mushrooms and drizzle balsamic sauce.  Sprinkle with chives.

**A dainty dish to serve your guests.**

**Fry skin side first, turn over when edges become whitish.**

**4** Thickening balsamic sauce

① Boil down balsamic vinegar with seasonings over low heat. At beginning, bubbles raise from bottom of pan.

② Sauce is ready when dark in color, and  liquid leaves a trail when dripped.

# CUTTLEFISH CUTLET

**Serves: 4**

10 oz(300 g) cuttlefish fillets
1 egg, beaten
1/4 cup water
1/3 cup(1 3/4 oz,50g) all-purpose flour
2 sprigs parsley, minced
1/4 cup grated Parmesan cheese

**Breadcrumbs**

6 Tbsp mayonnaise
2 Tbsp ketchup
1 Tbsp soy sauce

Lettuce, shredded
Lemon, wedged
Vegetable oil for deep-frying

**1** Lay cuttlefish and make crisscross scores diagonally as shown. Turn over and repeat. This will prevent curling when fried.
**2** Combine egg, water, flour, parsley, and Parmesan cheese. Coat cuttlefish fillet with egg mixture, and roll in breadcrumbs.
**3** Heat oil and fry cutlet until golden. Drain oil.
**4** Combine mayonnaise, ketchup and soy sauce.
**5** Line a serving dish with shredded lettuce and place sliced cuttlefish cutlet on it. Serve hot with the sauce and lemon wedge.

## Prevent curling

Calamari tends to curl when cooked. To prevent this, make criss-cross scores over both sides.

# MOROMIYAKI CHICKEN

**Serves: 4**

2/3 lb(300 g) boneless chicken
3 1/2 oz(100 g) moromi- miso
2"(5cm) length carrot
3 stalks scallion
1/2 stalk celery

**1** Cut chicken into thin, bite-size pieces.
**2** Spread moromi-miso (save some for vegetable strips) over bottom of a shallow container, and cover with a cheesecloth. Place chicken slices. Cover with cheesecloth and spread moromi-miso again. Let stand about 2 hours. This way chicken will not scorch when grilled.
**3** Cut carrot and celery into 1"(2.5cm) long julienne strips. Cut scallions into same size.
**4** Heat a gridiron and grill both sides until partially browned.
**5** Serve garnished with fresh vegetable strips.

Recycle used *moromi-miso*

Using a pestle, grind until smooth, and blend with same amount of white miso.

Cheesecloth between *miso* and chicken prevents *miso* from sticking to chicken.

# FRIED SCALLOPS

**Serves: 4**

8 scallops for *sashimi*
  All-purpose flour for dusting
  Beaten egg
  Breadcrumbs
Vegetable oil for deep-frying
1 2/3 oz(50 g) *Haccho-miso*
1 Tbsp grated onion
1/3 cup *dashi* stock
2 Tbsp heavy cream
Several cabbage leaves
  4 Tbsp rice vinegar
  1 Tbsp sugar
  Salt and pepper

and inside is still soft, as shown.

**3** Make *miso* sauce. In a saucepan, heat *dashi* stock, *Haccho-miso* and grated onion to a boil. Stir in heavy cream.

**4** Cook cut up cabbage leaves in boiling water (or in a microwave oven). Combine vinegar, sugar, salt and pepper in a bowl. Add cabbage and toss.

**5** Line a serving dish with cabbage. Place fried scallops and serve with *miso* sauce.

**1**
For dry and crisp coating, sprinkle container with breadcrumbs and place coated scallops.

**2**
If using fresh scallops for *sashimi*, leave center uncooked. Remove from oil quickly and let stand. remaining heat cook.

**1** Dust scallops with flour, coat with beaten egg, and roll in breadcrumbs. Sprinkle a shallow container sparingly with breadcrumbs, and lay prepared scallops. This way coating will not become soggy, resulting in crisp and dry outside.

**2** In 340°F(170 °C) oil, deep-fry briefly until outside is crisp

# BROCCOLI AND SHRIMP OMELET

**Serves: 4**

5 oz(150 g) shrimp, shelled
1/2 head broccoli,cut up
3 1/2 oz(100 g) white fish paste
4 Tbsp *Tamago no moto* (see p.27)
1 egg
*Kezuribushi* (bonito shavings)
Mayonnaise and soy sauce

**1** Cook deveined shrimp in boiling water as shown.

**2** In a medium bowl, combine *tamago no moto* and fish paste until smooth. (*Tamago no moto* can be substituted with mayonnaise.) Stir in beaten egg.

**3** Add shrimp and broccoli. Fold in lightly. Heat a non-stick skillet and drop shrimp

mixture to make 2"(5cm) rounds. As they scorch easily, cook over medium low heat just until heated through.

**4** Mix mayonnaise, soy sauce and *kezuribushi* and pour over omelets.

**1**

**Do not cook shrimp completely at this point. Rest of cooking will be done later.**

42

# STEAMED CHICKEN AND *SHIITAKE*

**1** Peel lemon thickly as shown. Slice thinly.
**2** Slice chicken thinly, by working knife at a slant.
**3** Lay about 10"(30 cm) aluminum foil. In center, layer *shiitake*, chicken and lemon slices alternately as shown.
**4** Bring up foil slightly so sauce will not spill out. Place butter on top and pour over soy sauce and *sake* mixture evenly.
**5** Bring up near and far ends of foil, and fold as shown.
**6** Fold up sides as shown. Cook in an oven preheated to 400°F (200 °C) 10 minutes or until chicken is cooked.

Trim away pulp completely as it gives bitterness.

Layer *shiitake*, chicken and lemon in order, sliding a little.

**Serves: 4**

2/3 lb(350g) chicken thigh
12 *shiitake* mushrooms
1 lemon
2 Tbsp butter

**Cooking Sauce**
{ 3 Tbsp soy sauce
4 Tbsp *sake*

Fold down edges twice to secure.

Fold in sides, pressing lightly. Check stability before placing in oven.

# CLEAR SOUP WITH MUSHROOMS

**Serves: 4**

1 package (3 1/3 oz,100g) *maitake* mushroom
1 package (3 1/3 oz,100g) *shimeji* mushrooms
1 package (3 1/3 oz,100g) *enokidake* mushrooms
1 package (3 1/3 oz,100g) *nameko* mushrooms
5 cups *dashi* stock
1/4 cup *sake*
1/2 cup *mirin*
1/2 cup soy sauce
*Mitsuba* (trefoil) or scallion

**1** Separate mushrooms into small segments. Cut *enokidake* in to half length.
**2** Parboil *nameko* as shown right.

**3** Heat all liquid ingredients to a boil. First add *nameko*, then *maitake* and *shimeji*, ending with *enokidake*. Cook only until heated through; turn off heat.
**4** Serve hot, sprinkled with *mitsuba* or scallion pieces.

Blanch *nameko* in boiling water and drain to remove extra stickiness.

# OTHER ASIAN TAPAS

Here are some enticing tapas dishes from our neighboring countries,
China, Korea and Taiwan,
that are sure to stimulate your appetite for both munching and drinking.
Just pick up the key seasonings and enjoy these quick and easy recipes
for casual gatherings or drinking parties with your friends.

# ASSORTED VEGETABLES (NAMOOL)

**Serves: 4**
**Fiddlehead Namool**
7 oz(200 g) fiddlehead
- 1 Tbsp toasted sesame seed
- 1 tsp sesame oil
- 2 Tbsp soy sauce
- 1/2 Tbsp salt

**Spinach Namool**
2/3 lb(300 g) spinach
- 1/2 Tbsp toasted sesame seed
- 1/2 Tbsp sesame oil
- 1/4 Tbsp MSG
- 1/3 tsp salt

**Bean Sprout Namool**
1 package bean sprouts
Scallions, sliced
- 1 Tbsp toasted sesame seed
- 1/2 Tbsp sesame oil
- 1/4 Tbsp MSG
- 1/2 tsp salt

**_Daikon_ Namool**
4"(10 cm) piece _daikon_ radish
2"(5 cm) piece carrot
- 5 Tbsp rice vinegar
- 3 Tbsp sugar
- 1/2 Tbsp salt

**Namool is an assortment of cooked vegetables in Korean flavor, featuring sesame seed and sesame oil.**

# Fiddlehead Namool

**1** Rinse cooked fiddlehead, and cook in boiling water until tender, and blanch in cold water; drain.
**2** In a skillet, heat vegetable oil, soy sauce, and salt until warm, and add fiddlehead, sesame seed and sesame oil. Cook briefly until liquid is absorbed.

# Spinach Namool

**1** Wash spinach, trim away root ends, and cut in half.
**2** Heat ample water to boil, and cook spinach only briefly.
**3** Plunge into water, and squeeze out moisture. Combine sesame seeds, sesame oil, MSG and salt in a bowl. Toss well.

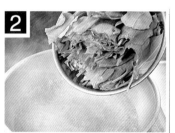

**Add spinach to boiling water. Do not overcook.**

# Daikon Namool

**1** Peel _daikon_ and carrot. Shred finely.
**2** Combine dressing ingredients and add to _daikon_ and carrot. Toss well.

# Bean Sprout Namool

**1** Rinse bean sprouts and cook in covered water. Blanch in cold water and drain in a colander.
**2** In a bowl, place bean sprouts and sliced scallions. Combine dressing ingredients and add to bowl. Toss well.

**Begin with water to cook bean sprouts. Don't overcook.**

**Bibimbap, a popular one-dish meal, is made of 4 kinds namools, sliced thin omelette, fresh egg yolk, and _nori_ seaweed, all arranged on cooked rice. Kochu jang and toasted sesame seed are added as condiments.**

# SHRIMP IN CHILI SAUCE

Spicy sauce enhances the springy shrimp. Great with drinks. Be sure to cook quickly over very high heat.

**Serves:** 4

30 shrimp

**Marinade for shrimp**

⎧ 1 tsp egg white, beaten
⎨ 1 tsp *sake*
⎩ Salt and pepper

1 1/2 Tbsp cornstarch

Vegetable oil

3 Tbsp sliced green onion

1 Tbsp grated ginger

1 Tbsp grated garlic

1/2 tsp toban jang
   (hot bean paste)

1/2 cup chicken stock

5 Tbsp ketchup

1 Tbsp sugar

Pinch salt

1 tsp cornstarch, dissolved in
   water

1/2 Tbsp chili oil

1/2 Tbsp sesame oil

1 Shell shrimp, pulling out tails. Devein. Marinate 10 minutes and stir in cornstarch to coat.

2 Heat a wok very hot, pour in vegetable oil, and deep-fry shrimp at 350°F(180℃). Remove from oil when shrimp start reddening.

3 Heat wok again. Add 3 Tbsp vegetable oil and heat until hot. Stir-fry grated garlic, ginger, toban jang, and green onion. Stir in chicken stock, ketchup, sugar and salt.

4 Add shrimp, followed by dissolved cornstarch, stirring quickly. Stir in chili oil and sesame oil.

In a bowl, place shrimp and pour in marinade.

In a preheated wok, deep-fry marinated shrimp until color turns red.

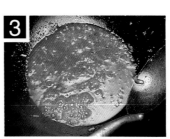

First stir-fry herbs and spices in heated oil. Then add stock and seasonings.

Stir in shrimp, then dissolved cornstarch to thicken sauce. Swirl in chili oil and sesame oil to enhance aroma.

# CHICKEN AND CASHEW NUTS

## Serves: 2

2 chicken thigh
1/2 cup unsalted cashew nuts
1 Japanese-type cucumber
1 pod red chili pepper
1 Tbsp oyster sauce
3 Tbsp chicken stock
1 tsp grated garlic
1 tsp cornstarch, dissolved in
   water

1/3 Tbsp *sake*
All-purpose flour
Vegetable oil

**1** Dice chicken into 1/2"
(1.5cm) cubes. Cut cucumber
into slightly smaller pieces.
Deep-fry cashew nuts until
crisp, but do not brown.
**2** Dust chicken cubes with
flour and deep-fry in 350°F
(180°C) oil until golden.
**3** Heat vegetable oil and fry
grated garlic. Stir in oyster
sauce. Add chicken and
cucumber. Stir in chicken
stock, *sake* and dissolved
cornstarch. Cook and stir until
thickened.
**4** Add cashew nuts and
chopped chili pepper. Stir
quickly and transfer to a
serving dish. Serve while nuts
are crunchy.

Enjoy irresitible crunchiness of fried
cashew nuts with flavorful chicken.

Prepare ingredients. Deep-fry
cashew nuts and cut chicken
and cucumber into cubes.

Dust chicken and deep-fry
until golden brown.

Do not add cashew nuts
until the last minute.

when nuts and chili
pepper are stirred in,
remove from heat.

# MARINATED CLAMS

**Serves: 2**

2/3 lb(300 g) fresh water clams
4 cups water
5 pods red chili peppers
1 knob ginger root
1 clove garlic
150 ml soy sauce
100 ml *sake*
100 ml *mirin*

**Try with any kind of fresh clams.**

**1** Clean clam shells, rubbing each other in water. Thinly slice ginger root, and crush garlic.

**2** In a skillet, place clams and cold water. Cook over low heat 20 minutes. Drain in a colander, reserving cooking liguid.

**3** In a bowl place clams, cooking water, chili peppers, garlic and ginger. Add all seasonings and mix. Cover and refrigerate one day.

**4** Serve with some of marinade.

# GARLIC SAUTEED BOK CHOY

**Serves: 2**

2 bok choy
2 tsp grated garlic
3 Tbsp vegetable oil
Dash chicken stock
1 tsp MSG
4 tsp salt

**Refreshing sauteed greens to be served as a side to anything.**

**1** Cut bok choy leaves into 3"(7.5 cm) pieces, and slice stalks thinly as shown.

**2** Heat vegeatable oil in a skillet. Fry grated garlic so as to release aroma.

**3** Add bok choy and stir-fry until the color turns brilliant green.

**4** Stir in dash chicken stock, MSG, and salt. Cook only briefly to retain crispness of stalks.

Prepare ingredients. Slice ginger root and crush garlic cloves.

Cook clams over low heat, with water to cover partially.

Cut bok choy leaves into 3"(7.5cm) pieces, and slice stalks thinly.

Don't overcook, to retain crispness of stalks.

# BEEF AND GARLIC SHOOTS

### Serves: 4

1/2 lb (230 g)  lean beef
1/2 lb (230 g)  garlic shoots
1/4 lb (120 g)  bamboo shoot
**Marinade**
⎡ 1 tsp beaten egg
⎜ 1 tsp *sake*
⎜ Salt and pepper
⎣ 1 1/2 Tbsp  cornstarch
Vegetable oil for deep-frying
**Cooking Sauce**
⎡ 1 Tbsp *sake*
⎜ 1 tsp  sugar
⎜ 1 Tbsp soy sauce
⎜ 1 tsp  rice vinegar
⎜ 1/2 tsp MSG
⎜ 1 tsp  cornstarch
⎣ Dash red chili pepper,chopped
1 Tbsp  sesame oil

**1** Cut beef into julienne strips. Combine marinade ingredients and add beef strips. Set aside.
**2** Cut bamboo shoot into same size strips as beef, and garlic shoots into 3"(7.5cm) engths.
**3** In a wok, heat 3 cups vegetable oil to 350°F(180°C), and blanch garlic shoots, bamboo shoot, then beef; drain and empty wok.
**4** In a bowl, combine sauce ingredients.
**5** Heat wok again.  Cook and stir blanched beef and vegetables with sauce as shown.
**6** Swirl in sesame oil and stir to fold in.

Add in order: garlic shoots, bamboo shoot, then beef. Stir in combined sauce ingredients at a time.

# SPICY PORK SALAD

### Serves: 4

1/4 lb (120 g)  pork loin, thinly
    sliced
1/4 lb (120 g)   Chinese roast
    pork
1/4 lb (120 g)  steamed chicken
    breast
1 Japanese-type cucumber
1 medium tomato
4" (10 cm) length green onion
**Spicy Dressing**
⎡ 2 Tbsp soy sauce
⎜ 1 tsp  sugar
⎜ 1 Tbsp rice vinegar
⎣ 2 Tbsp sesame oil
⎡ 1/2 tsp grated garlic
⎜ 1 tsp hot bean paste
⎣ Dash chili oil

**1** Boil pork slices and cut into bite-size pieces.
**2** Slice Chinese roast pork thinly. Tear steamed chicken into thin strips.
**3** Prepare cucumber as shown.
**4** Cut cracked cucumber diagonal pieces.
**5** Cut tomato into wedges, then cut diagonally in half. Slice green onion into julienne strips.
**6** In a bowl, place meats and vegetables. Combine dressing ingredient somitting garlic, hot bean paste and chili oil, and add to bowl. Toss well, then add remaining seasonings. Mix well.

Cut cucumber in half. Using a side of knife, pound to make cracks so flavor will penetrate.

49

# SPRING ROLLS

## Serves: 4

10 spring roll wrappers
1 oz (30 g) sliced pork
10 oz (300 g) sliced vegetables
   including cabbage, bamboo
   shoot, *enokidake* mushrooms,
   green onion, ginger root

(A)
- 1 tsp *sake*
- 1 Tbsp soy sauce
- 1 tsp sugar

1/2 cup chicken stock
1 Tbsp cornstarch
1 tsp sesame oil
Vegetable oil for deep-frying

**1** Cut pork and vegetables into julienne strips. Heat about 3 cups vegetable oil to 350°F (180°C) in a wok, and blanch them; immediately drain and empty wok.

**2** In wok, return blanched pork and vegetables, and add seasonings (A) and chicken stock. Heat to a boil, stir in dissolved cornstarch and sprinkle with sesame oil.

**3** Transfer thickened filling into a shallow container and cool in refrigerator.

**4** Wrap filling as shown, and deep-fry until golden. Serve hot.

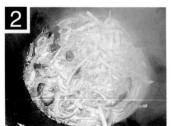

Stir-fry blanched filling ingredients with seasonings, then thicken with dissolved cornstarch.

Place filling near center of wrapper. Fold up near end, and fold in sides. Roll up and seal with beaten egg.

# FRIED CHICKEN CARTILAGE

## Serves: 4

1/2 lb(230g) triangular chicken
   cartilage

**Batter**
- 2 tsp beaten egg
- 1 Tbsp cornstarch
- 1 tsp *sake*
- Salt and pepper to taste
- Dash MSG

Vegetable oil for deep-frying

**1** In a bowl, place cartilage and coat with beaten egg. Add *sake*, MSG, salt and pepper. Add cornstarch and mix well in a kneading motion.

**2** Heat 3 cups of oil to 350°F (180°C). Deep-fry until golden brown.

**3** Serve with chili pepper and mayonnaise, if desired.

**These exceptionally crunchy and tasty morsels are a specialty of *izakaya*, and not of restaurants.**

Coat cartilage with beaten egg, toss with seasonings, then "knead" with cornstarch.

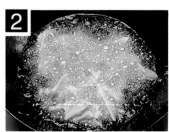

Preheat wok or skillet hot so batter won't stick to bottom.

# POT STICKERS

**Serves: 4**
20 jiaozi wrappers
**Filling**
- 2 1/2 oz (70 g) ground pork
- 3 1/2 oz (100 g) pork fat
- 1/4 head cabbage, minced
  (1/2 tsp salt for cabbage)
- 2 oz (60g) garlic chives
- 2" (5cm) length  green onion
- 1 Tbsp grated garlic
- 1 Tbsp grated ginger root
- 1 tsp each *sake*, sugar
- 1 Tbsp soy sauce
- 2 Tbsp sesame oil
Vegetable oil for frying

**1** Knead cabbage with salt until supple.  Rinse with water and squeeze.

**2** In a bowl, mix ground pork, minced fat and cabbage using your fingers. Add *sake*, sugar, soy sauce, salt and "knead" well. Mince garlic chives and green onion and add to bowl. Mix in all remaining ingredients andl.

**3** Wrap filling with jiaozi wrappers as shown, making pleats if preferred.

**4** Heat vegetable oil in a skillet, pack wrapped jiaozi. When bottoms are browned, pour over water to almost cover. Cover and let steam over high heat until water is evaporated. When bottoms are crisp, transfer onto serving dish (upside down) .

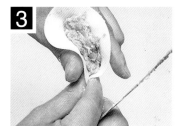

**Place about 1 Tbsp filling in center of wrapper. Press lightly and pinch moistened ends.**

# JIAOZI SOUP

**Serves: 4**
20 wonton wrappers (square)
**Filling** (see left)
**Soup**
- 2-3 leaves  garlic chives
- 1/4 stalk  green onion
- 1 cup  chicken stock
- 2 1/3 Tbsp light soy sauce
- Freshly ground black pepper

**Smooth and slippery outside and juicy inside make a great contrast.**

**1** Center about 1 Tbsp filling on each wrapper. Fold in half, then close edges as shown.

**2** Bring 4 cups water to a boil. Cook jiaozi until they float to surface, about 4 minutes.

**3** Add sliced garlic chives and green onion, chicken stock, light soy sauce, and pepper. Stir to blend. Transfer into individual serving bowls.

**Fold stuffed wrapper into a triangle, and close edges by folding pleats from sides, if you prefer.**

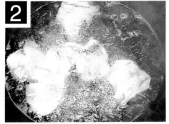

**Cook 4 minutes or until all jiaozi float to surface.**

# PORK AND EGGS

**Enjoy the contrast of fluffy omelet and crunchy textures of bamboo shoot and fungi.**

### Serves: 4

1/4 lb(120 g) lean pork

**Marinade**

> 1 tsp beaten egg
> 1 tsp *sake*
> MSG, salt and pepper
> 1 1/2 Tbsp cornstarch

1 bamboo shoot, boiled
1 oz (30g) snow peas
1 oz (30g) softened cloud ears
4 eggs, beaten
1 tsp *sake*
1/2 tsp sugar
1 Tbsp soy sauce
Dash MSG and pepper
1 tsp sesame oil
Vegetable oil

**1** Slice pork thinly, then into julienne strips. Place in a bowl and coat with marinade excluding cornstarch. Lastly coat with cornstarch. Cut bamboo shoot likewise. Cut up cloud ear fungi. String snow peas.

**2** Heat extra vegetable oil(about 3 cups) in a wok until hot, and blanch prepared meat and vegetables only briefly; drain as shown right.

**3** Reheat wok with 2 Tbsp oil and stir in beaten eggs. Just before eggs are set, add cooked meat and vegetables and stir-fry quickly.

**4** Season with *sake*, sugar, soy sauce, MSG and pepper. Stir in sesame oil and remove from heat.

**Note:** It is a basic Chinese cooking technique to marinate meats and to precook vegetables before stir-frying together.

Marinated meat and prepared vegetables. Soften cloud ear by soaking in hot water 15 minutes.

Blanch briefly in hot oil in an order: pork, bamboo shoot, snow peas, then cloud ears, adding to a colander.

Heat oil in wok and stir-fry beaten eggs until fluffy and almost cooked.

Add precooked meat and vegetables, and stir in seasonings. Finish with sesame oil swirled in.

# FISH AND *TOFU* CASSEROLE

Korea's most popular winter hot pot, cooked on the table.

## Serves: 3

1/2 codfish (about 2/3 lb,300 g)
6 prawns
1/4 root *daikon* radish, sliced
1/4 onion, sliced
1 cake *tofu*, sliced
1/2 stalk green onion, sliced
1 package *enokidake* mushrooms
1 bunch edible chrysanthemums

**To season broth**
  1/2 Tbsp grated garlic
  1/2 Tbsp hot bean paste
  2/3 Tbsp *dashi* powder
  1/2 Tbsp MSG
  2/3 Tbsp salt
  Dash pepper

**Hint:** Do not add all at a time. Save tender vegetables for last so everything will be ready at the same time. Do not overboil and constantly skim foams that float.

**1** Slice *daikon* into 3/4"(2 cm) rounds, then crosswise into 1/4"(6mm) strips. Cut up cod. Half fill a fireproof casserole with water, and add cod, prawns, *daikon* and onion. Cook over medium heat.

**2** Bring to a boil and add *tofu* and green onion. Continue to cook.

**3** Skim floating bubbles. Trim *enokidake* mushrooms and add to pot.

**4** Finally add greens and heat through.

In a fire-proof casserole, heat water, codfish, prawns, *daikon* and onion to boiling.

Add *tofu* and green onion. Simmer over low heat.

While simmering, remove floating bubbles constantly.

Add chrysanthemum leaves and simmer until heated through.

# BASIL AND TOMATO CHICKEN

Appetizing fried chicken with tangy tomato and basil sauce.

## Serves: 2

6-8 （1/2 lb,230g)boneless
   chicken wings

**Marinade**

- 1 Tbsp soy sauce
- 1 Tbsp sesame oil
- 1 Tbsp *sake*
- 1 Tbsp grated garlic
- Dash pepper

Cornstarch for dusting
1 medium tomato
6 basil leaves
1 tsp grated garlic
1 Tbsp butter
1 tsp cornstarch
1 1/2 Tbsp *sake*
1 tsp sesame oil
1 tsp vegetable oil
4 Tbsp chicken stock
Dash MSG and salt
Vegetable oil for deep-frying

**1** Combine marinade ingredients. Add chicken and rub well as shown. Let stand 20 minutes at room temperature.

**2** Cut marinated chicken wings into halves. Dust with cornstarch and deep-fry in 350°F (180℃ ) oil about 6 minutes.

**3** Heat 1 Tbsp vegetable oil and fry grated garlic to release aroma. Peel and cup up tomato. Add to skillet with butter. Saute briefly.

**4** Add chicken stock and reduce heat to low. Stir in cornstarch dissolved in same amount of water to thicken sauce. Add fried chicken pieces, return heat to medium. Cook and stir with basil leaves, *sake* and sesame oil. Season with MSG and salt.

Rub chicken with marinade, using your fingers.

Dust marinated chicken pieces with cornstarch, and deep-fry until golden.

Saute grated garlic, then tomato in vegetable oil and butter.

Reduce heat and add fried chicken pieces. Stir in basil leaves and seasonings.

# MAPO *TOFU* KOREAN STYLE

**Serves: 2**

1 cake soft *tofu*, diced
1 1/2 Tbsp ground pork
6-8 baby clams, boiled
1/2 stalk green onion
1 egg, beaten
1/3 Tbsp MSG
2/3 Tbsp *dashi* powder
Dash chili pepper
4 cups water

**1** In a greased 8"(20 cm) fireproof pot, stir-fry ground pork over medium heat.
**2** Add *tofu* and bring to a boil. Season with MSG and *dashi* powder. Add clams, sliced green onion and chili pepper. Cook until flavors areabsorbed. Stir in beaten egg and return to boil.

**Note:** Adjust spiciness with chili pepper.

# *DAIKON* OMELET

**Serves: 2**

1 1/4 oz (40 g) dried *daikon* radish strips
3 eggs
Dash salt and MSG
1 Tbsp vegetable oil

**1** Soften dried *daikon* strips by soaking in ample water 30 minutes, and cut up.
**2** In a bowl, mix *daikon*, eggs, salt and MSG.
**3** Heat vegetable oil in a skillet, and pour in egg mixture all at once. Do not stir. Turn over and fry until golden on both sides.

**Note:** To make a fluffy omelet, be sure to beat the eggs well until everly textured. Also, be careful so as not to overcook and harden the omelet.

Fry ground meat and reduce heat so as not to boil.

When all ingredients are added, stir in beaten egg and continue to cook.

Mix dried *daikon*, eggs, MSG, and salt until well blended.

Heat vegetable oil and fry both sides until golden brown.

# SCALLOPS AND BROCCOLI

Broccoli, carrot and scallops make a colorful combo, cooked in a delicate sauce.

### Serves: 2

1 head broccoli
3"(8 cm) length carrot
5 oz(150 g) small scallops
100 ml chicken stock
1 Tbsp cornstarch
1 Tbsp sesame oil

### Hints on preparation

Cut carrot crosswise into halves, and make 5 V-shape incisions around edges. Slice thinly to form flowers. Broccoli will turn bright green if a few drops of vegetable oil are

sprinkled into boiling water. Vegetables are parboiled so as to shorten the stir-frying time.

**1** Separate broccoli into florets. Cook broccoli and sliced carrot flowers in boiling water only briefly; set aside.
**2** Heat chicken stock to a boil and stir in cornstarch dissolved in same amount of water to thicken. Add salt, MSG and sugar to season.
**3** Return to boil, and add scallops. Cook and stir over high heat.
**4** Add broccoli and carrot flowers. Cook and stir until heated through. Sprinkle sesame oil and remove from heat.

Parboil broccoli florets and carrot flowers in boiling water, only to heat through; set aside.

Heat chicken stock to a boil and thicken with dissolved cornstarch.

First add scallops. Stir to cook evenly.

Add vegetables and stir to heat through. Return to boil and add sesame oil.

# CALAMARI AND CELERY

Irresistible resilience of calamari and celery is the secret of this popular Chinese dish that goes well with drinks.

## Serves: 2

1 large calamari
6 cloud ears, softened
1 stalk celery
1/3 medium carrot
1/2 stalk green onion, sliced
5 Tbsp chicken stock
1 1/2 Tbsp cornstarch
1 tsp *sake*
1 tsp sesame oil
Dash salt and MSG

**1** Pull out inside of calamari and discard. Cut calamari body lengthwise to open flat. Remove skin holding edge with a paper towel. Make crisscross scores over surface working your knife at a slant. Cut into 4"(10cm) long rectangles as shown.

**2** Remove tough strings from celery and cut into 3"(7.5 cm) diagonal slices. Slice carrot into flowers (see opposite page for preparation). In boiling water, cook softened cloud ears, celery and carrot.

**3** Add calamari, and turn off heat immediately to prevent overcooking; drain in a colander.

**4** Combine chicken stock and cornstarch, and heat to thicken, stirring constantly. Slice green onion and add to pan together with calamari, cloud ears, celery and carrot, all at a time. Stir-fry quickly so as to coat with thick sauce.

**5** Stir in *sake* and sesame oil. Adjust taste with salt and MSG.

To absorb flavor, make scores over flattened calamari. Use knife at a slant.

Parboil ear fungi, celery and carrot.

In same pan, parboil cut-up calamari only for a second. Remove from heat immediately and drain.

Stir-fry all ingredients quickly over high heat, and season to taste.

57

# KOREAN PANCAKES

## Potato Pancakes

**Serves: 2**

1 potato
  1/4 Tbsp all-purpose flour
  1/2 Tbsp *dashi* powder
  1/4 Tbsp MSG
6 edible chrysanthemum or coriander
Vegetable oil for frying

**1** Peel and grate potato. Drain in a colander to discard liquid. Combine drained potato with flour and seasonings.
**2** In a skillet, heat vegetable oil and spoon potato mixture into skillet. Press down into about 3"(7.5 cm) rounds as shown. Turn over and fry until browned on both sides. Garnish with chrysanthemum leaves.

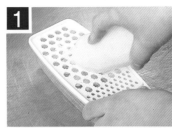

Grate potato and discard liquid.

Form into rounds and saute both sides.

## Seafood Pancake

(pictured above right)

**Serves: 3**

1 calamari tentacles
Half a dozen oysters
1 oz (60 g) scallions
1/4 onion, chopped
1/4 carrot, shredded
**(A)**
  ⌈ 1 egg, beaten
  │ 1 1/4 Tbsp all-purpose flour
  │ 1 1/4 Tbsp cornstarch
  │ 1/2 Tbsp *dashi* powder
  ⌊ 1/4 Tbsp MSG

**Dip**
  ⌈ 2/3 Tbsp soy sauce
  ⌊ 1/3 Tbsp rice vinegar
Vegetable oil for frying

**1** In a bowl, combine ingredients **(A)**.
**2** Cut calamari tentacles into 3/8"(1 cm) pieces, and add to bowl. Cut scallions into 1"(2.5 cm) lengths and add to bowl. Add onion and carrot. Mix lightly just to fold.
**3** Heat vegetable oil in a skillet, and spread calamari mixture and press down flat. Dot with halved oysters. Cook over low heat.
**4** Turn over to fry both sides, but do not brown.
**5** Transfer to a serving dish and cut into pieces. Serve with vinegar soy sauce as a dip.

Press flat in a skillet and dot with halved oysters.

## Kimchee Pancake

**Serves: 3**

10 oz (300 g) Chinese cabbage kimchee
5 Tbsp all-purpose flour
1/4 Tbsp MSG
Vegetable oil

**1** Shred kimchee finely. In a bowl, combine kimchee, flour, MSG, 2 Tbsp oil and water. Mix but do not stir until gluey.
**2** Heat oil in a skillet and spread dough, pressing down to flatten. Do not brown.

Mix kimchee, flour, MSG, and oil until well blended.

Heat oil in a skillet. Fry both sides over low heat.

# SPICY *DAIKON* RADISH

## Serves: 4

3 1/3lb(1.5kg) *daikon* radish
　5 Tbsp salt
3 rice flour
**Marinade**

> 1 stalk green onion, minced
> 1/2 onion, minced
> 3 Tbsp salted opossum shrimp
> 1/2 Tbsp grated garlic
> 1/2 Tbsp grated gingerroot
> 2 Tbsp nam pla (fish sauce)
> 5 Tbsp Korean chili powder
> 1/2 tsp MSG

**1** Cut *daikon* into 1"(2.5 cm) dices.

**2** In a bowl, place *daikon* and salt. Mix well until salt is dissolved. Pour over boiling water and drain. Let stand. Rinse and drain.

**3** Dissolve rice flour with little water, and combine with marinade ingredients well.

**4** Add *daikon* and mix to coat as shown, and marinate in refrigerator about a week.

# *TOFU* STEAK

## Serves: 2

1 cake *tofu*, drained
2 eggs, beaten
1/4 tsp salt
1/4 Tbsp MSG
**Piquant Sauce**

> 2　Tbsp　soy sauce
> 1/2　Tbsp　sesame oil
> 1/2　Tbsp　Korean chili
> 　　　　　powder
> 2　Tbsp　sliced scallions
> 1　Tbsp　grated carrot
> 1/2　Tbsp　sesame seed

Vegetable oil for frying

**1** Slice *tofu* into 3/8"(1 cm) thicknesses.

**2** Add salt and MSG to beaten eggs, and stir until blended. Add *tofu* slices and mix to coat well.

**3** Heat vegetable oil hot, and fry coated *tofu* over medium low heat.

**4** Turn over when golden, to cook both sides.

**5** Combine piquant sauce ingredients and pour over steaming *tofu* steaks.

Pour boiling water over salted *daikon*, drain and let stand 1.5 hours.

Mix *daikon* with marinade. Marinate at least 1 week for the best flavor.

In a hot and greased skillet, fry egg-coated *tofu* slices.

Turn over to cook both sides until golden.

# JELLYFISH SALAD

## Serves: 3

10 oz (300 g) salted jellyfish
**Dressing**
   1/4 Tbsp grated garlic
   1/2 Tbsp hot mustard paste
   5 Tbsp rice vinegar
   2 Tbsp sugar
2 sticks krab fish cake
1/2 Japanese-type cucumber
White peppercorns to taste

**Crunchy jellyfish salad is a must in Chinese appetizers.**

**1** Soak jellyfish in water and blanch in hot water(see p.20). Drain and cut up.
**2** On a serving dish, place jellyfish in a heap, and top with separated krab fish cake and cucumber strips. Combine dressing ingredients and pour over jellyfish.
**3** Serve sprinkled with peppercorns, and toss on the table.

# VINEGARED LOTUS ROOT

## Serves: 3

1 lb(450 g) lotus root
**Marinade**
   1 pod red chili pepper, sliced
   1 tsp sesame oil
   1 tsp *sake*
   1 tsp MSG
   1 tsp salt
   2 tsp sugar
   1 lemon, squeezed

**1** Wash lotus root using a brush under running water. In boiling water cook, whole root

2-3 minutes. Overcooking spoils crisp texture.
**2** Drain water and let stand to cool in pan.
**3** In a bowl, combine marinade ingredients. Peel and slice cooled lotus root and add to bowl. Using your fingers, rub on marinade so lotus root will absorb flavor well.
**4** Cover with a plastic wrap and refrigerate 1 hour before serving.

**1**

In a bowl, wash jellyfish in water, and soak in clear water.

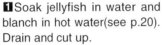
**2**

Heap jellyfish topped with fish cake and cucumber strips. Pour over dressing.

**1**

Cook cleaned lotus root in boiling water, just to heat through.

**3**

Slice lotus root into half moon slices, and rub on marinade.

# MARINATED CUCUMBERS

## FRIED CHICKEN GIZZARDS

### Serves: 3

3 Japanese-type cucumbers
 3 tsp salt

**Marinade**
- 5 oz (150 g)  sugar
- 200 ml rice vinegar
- 1/3 Tbsp toban jang (hot bean paste)
- 2/3 Tbsp chili oil
- 1/3 oz (10 g)  sliced ginger root
- 2/3 oz (20 g)  shredded carrot

**1** Quarter cucumber lengthwise and trim away seeds as shown. Cut into 2"(5 cm) lengths.

**2** In a bowl, rub cucumbers with measured salt until supple.

**3** Rinse in water to remove extra saltiness. Combine marinade ingredients and add cucumbers. Toss well. Cover with a plastic wrap and refrigerate overnight until flavors are absorbed.

### Serves: 3

2/3 lb (300g) chicken gizzards

**Marinade**
- 1 Tbsp soy sauce
- 1 Tbsp sesame oil
- 1 Tbsp *sake*
- 1 Tbsp grated garlic
- Pepperto taste

Cornstarch for dusting
Vegetable oil for deep-frying
Salt and pepper

### Delicious, garlic-flavored morsels.

**1** Halve chicken gizzards and make crisscross incisions on each, to absorb flavor.

**2** In a bowl, combine gizzards and marinade ingredients and mix, rubbing with your fingers. Let stand 20 minutes until flavors are absorbed.

**3** Coat gizzards with cornstarch. Heat oil to 480°F (250°C). Add gizzards and immediately reduce heat. Deep-fry about 4 minutes. Serve, sprinkled with salt and pepper.

**1** Work your knife horizontally to trim away center seeds.

**2** Using your fingers, rub salt on cucumber strips until supple.

**1** Halve chicken gizzards and make incisions so as to absorb marinade quickly.

**3** Dust marinated gizzards with cornstarch, and add to hot oil, reducing heat immediately.

# RICE GRUEL WITH SEAFOOD

**Easy to digest, rice gruel is quite filling yet extremely low in calorie, which is another reason of its popularity.**

**Serves: 4**

1 cup (1/2 lb, 230 g) cooked short grain rice

**Toppings:**

Shrimp, shelled
Clams in shell
Steamed chicken
Bok choy
Bamboo shoot
*Shiitake* mushroom

1 cup chicken stock
1/2 tsp *sake*
Salt and pepper to taste
1 Tbsp vegetable oil
Dash MSG
Fresh coriander

**1** Place cooked rice in a rice cooker. Pour in double amount of water and set "warm" 2-3 hours until volume increases as shown.

**2** Prepare toppings. Cut each into small cubes except for clams.

**3** In a wok or saucepan, heat chicken stock, clams and vegetable oil to a boil.

**4** When clams are opened, add swollen rice, *sake*, salt and MSG. Cook over low heat and add remaining toppings. Sprinkle with pepper and continue to cook about 3 minutes. Serve hot, garnished with coriander snips, if desired.

**Note:** This is a good way of using leftover cooked rice. Just warm rice with double amount of water for 3-4 hours, then voila, rice is so fluffy and moist, ready to eat as a simple rice gruel. This is a Chinese version cooked with toppings. Choose any toppings you fancy.

In a rice cooker, place leftover cooked rice and double amount of water. Set "warm" 3-4 hours.

Prepare seafood and vegetables of your choice by cutting into small cubes.

**Cook clams in chicken stock with vegetable oil until shells are open.**

**Add rice and season to taste. Continue to cook with toppings.**

# FRIED RICE WITH KIMCHEE

## Serves: 1

1 heap cup (2/3 lb, 300 g) cooked rice
3 oz (90 g) Chinese cabbage kimchee
1/2 Tbsp butter
1 tsp light soy sauce
1/4 Tbsp MSG
1 Tbsp white sesame seed
1 tsp sesame oil
1 egg
Vegetable oil for frying

**Note:** Spiciness of kimchee is softened by frying with butter. Besides, half-cooked egg yolk will enrich the flavor as well as making it milder. If you prefer, add some of kimchee marinade to rice when frying.

**1** Cut up kimchee without squeezing out marinade. Cook egg sunny-side up and set aside.
**2** In a preheated skillet, cook and stir kimchee with butter and MSG.
**3** Add rice and stir-fry so as to separate rice grains. Stir in light soy sauce.
**4** Add toasted sesame seed and sesame oil.
**5** Place in a serving dish, and top with egg sunny-side up.

**Place egg sunny-side up on top.**

Gourmet's secret: Serve topped with egg sunny-side up and mix with rice.

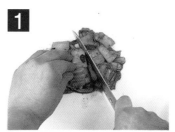

**Cut up kimchee without squeezing out marinade.**

**Cook and stir kimchee with butter and MSG.**

**Add rice and stir-fry so as to separate rice grains.**

**Sprinkle with toasted sesame seed and sesame oil, mix lightly.**

# FRIED RICE VERMICELLI

Healthy rice vermicelli is an ideal meal for "heavy" drinkers!

## Serves: 1

5 oz (150 g) rice vermicelli
1 3/4 oz (50 g) pork, sliced
1 3/4 oz (50 g) cabbage
1/2 oz (15 g)  dried *shiitake* mushrooms
1/10 oz (3 g)  dried shrimp
1/4 cup  chicken stock
Salt and pepper to taste

**1** Soften dried *shiitake* mushrooms in water 2-3 hours, then slice thinly. Cut pork and cabbage into julienne strips.
**2** Bring ample water to a boil and cook rice vermicelli 5 minutes; drain in a colander.
**3** Heat oil in skillet and stir-fry pork, cabbage, *shiitake* and shrimp.
**4** When pork turns whitish in color, pour in chicken stock, salt. Stir-fry over low heat.
**5** Add rice vermicelli, sprinkle with pepper, and stir-fry quickly over high heat.

**1** Prepare ingredients: shrimp, soften dried *shiitake* . Cut all into julienne strips.

Cook rice vermicelli in ample water; drain.

Stir-fry pork, cabbage, *shiitake* and shrimp.

Add chicken stock and salt to taste.

Stir in rice vermicelli and fry quickly over high heat.

# TAIWANESE NOODLES

This Taiwan's food stall specialty is gaining popularity in Japan because of the flavorful meat paste topping.

## Serves: 1

1 portion  Chinese noodles
4 stalks garlic chives
1/3 oz (10 g) bean sprouts
**Meat Paste**
- 5 oz(150 g)  boneless pork rib
- 3 1/2 oz (100g)  fried green onion*
- 1 3/4 oz (50 g)  green onion
- 1 knob ginger root
- 5 cloves garlic, grated
- 1 Tbsp lard
- 1 1/2 Tbsp soy sauce
- 2 Tbsp sesame oil
- 1 tsp sugar
- 1 tsp MSG

400 ml chicken stock
Pinch salt

*To make fried green onion, fry minced green onions slowly, until crisp.

**1** Prepare ingredients. Cut up pork. Mince green onion, and slice ginger root thinly.
**2** Melt lard in a skillet, and stir-fry grated garlic over low heat. Stir in fried green onion, sliced ginger root and soy sauce. Finally add pork and sesame oil. When meat turns color, add sugar and MSG. Continue to stir-fry over low heat.
**3** Heat ample water to a boil, and cook noodles, garlic chives and bean sprouts 1 minute; drain in a colander.
**4** Place cooked noodles in a serving bowl, and put bean sprouts and garlic chives in center. Pour heated chicken stock and top with meat paste. When eating, mix toppings with noodles.

Prepare meat and vegetables.

Fry grated garlic, then fried green onion, and ginger root.

Cook noodles with garlic chives and bean sprouts; drain.

Transfer to serving bowl, pour over stock and place meat paste on top.

# POPULAR ANTIPASTI
# PRIMI PIATTI

In Japan, Italian or French cuisine has never been so popular as it is today.
It is mainly because they are now served at inexpensive,
small restaurants in a relaxed atmosphere.
Antipasto actually originated as a means of preserving food,
so you can prepare days ahead for gatherings.
It is fun to discuss which drink would go best with which dish you share.

# BEEF CARPACCIO

**Serves: 4**

2 oz(60 g) fresh beef round
Parmigiano Reggiano
Arugula
Lemon juice
Virgin olive oil
Salt and pepper to taste

**1** Freeze beef and thaw partially so as to slice thinly.
**2** Cut into paper thin slices of about 1/8"(3mm).
**3** On a serving plate, spread beef slices. Cover with a plastic wrap and pound evenly with a bottle as shown.
**4** Swirl olive oil over spread beef, then sprinkle with salt, pepper and lemon juice.
**5** Slice Parmigiano Reggiano paper thin, using a cheese slicer, and place on beef.
**6** Top with roughly shredded arugula leaves.

This Italian tri-colored dish enhances the taste of white wine.

**Freeze beef right after purchasing. Thaw just before a knife is inserted.**

**Carefully slice beef while partially frozen.**

By covering beef slices with a plastic wrap, they will spread easily without sticking to the bottle.

**Season with olive oil, salt, pepper and lemon juice.**

**Parmigiano Reggiano will enrich the flavor of beef by layering over it.**

**Garnish with refreshing arugula leaves.**

# BRUSCHETTA

**Serves: 10**

1 lb (450 g) cream cheese
1 tsp  minced garlic
1 oz (30 g) raisins
2/3 oz (20 g) each, walnuts
   and pine nuts
Peppercorns
200 ml heavy cream
50 ml milk
Pinch salt

**1** Soften raisins by soaking in water. Also soften cream cheese leaving at room temperature. Roast walnuts and pine nuts in a skillet. Crush peppercorns using a hammer to release aroma.
**2** In a large bowl, stir cream cheese until smooth.  Add minced garlic and mix well.
**3** Add raisins, nuts and peppercorns and mix well. (Break walnuts using your hands)  Add heavy cream and milk.  Season with salt and refrigerate overnight.
**4** Toast thinly sliced French bugget, and spread cheese mixture in a heap.

# MARINATED HORSE MACKEREL

**Serves: 5**

4-5  horse mackerel
   Pinch salt
**Marinade**
   400 ml white wine vinegar
   100 ml white wine
   1 bay leaf
   1 sprig thyme
   1 clove garlic
   1 pod dried chili pepper
   2/3 tsp peppercorns
   1 slice lemon
   1 sprig parsley
   Olive oil

**1** In a saucepan, bring all marinade ingredients to a boil. Remove from heat and set aside to cool.
**2** Separate flesh of horse mackerel from backbone as shown. Sprinkle with salt, cover and refrigerate 30 minutes.
**3** Dry fish fillets  with paper towel, and marinate 1 hour, refrigerated.
**4** Pour over olive oil to cover fish fillets.  Let stand overnight at room temperature.

Prepare everything before mixing. Use any nuts such as roasted almond or peanut.

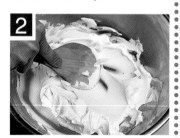

To smooth cream cheese, use a wooden spatula or food processor.

Bring marinade to a boil, and set aside to cool.

Discard head, inside and bones before rinsing in cold water.

Flavor will be best after a day. Keeps 1 week.

# CORNED BEEF GRATIN

# CLAMS BAKED IN GARLIC BUTTER

## Serves: 3

1 medium onion
3 cloves garlic, minced
5 medium tomatoes
Vegetable oil for frying
3 1/2 oz(100 g) corned beef
3 eggs
Salt and pepper to taste
Grated natural cheese
Minced parsley

**1** Mince onion. Dip tomatoes briefly in hot water and peel. Remove seeds and cut up.
**2** Fry minced garlic in hot oil until aroma is released. Add onion and fry until transparent, then cook tomatoes.
**3** Cook and stir over low heat until moisture evaporates. Season with salt and pepper.
**4** Transfer into a bowl, and break corned beef into it. Mix well.
**5** Place in a casserole and break an egg on top. Sprinkle with cheese and parsley. In 400°F(200°C) oven, bake until egg sets.

## Serves: 4

20 clams
White wine
**Garlic Butter**
　1/2 lb (230 g) butter
　3 tsp minced shallot
　1 Tbsp minced garlic
　1 1/2 Tbsp almond meal
　Lemon juice
　Salt and pepper
Rock salt, optional

**1** Insert a knife between shells of clam. Cut joints on both sides as shown.
**2** Open shell and scrape off flesh. Sprinkle with wine and set aside.
**3** On an oven-proof serving plate, place rock salt. Arrange shells refilled with clams on it. Stir all garlic butter ingredients and pipe or spoon onto clams.
**4** Bake in oven preheated to 400°F(200°C) until surface is dry.

Be sure to cut into joints on both sides to separate flesh from shell completely.

Use tip of knife to scrape out flesh.

Pipe or spoon garlic butter generusly onto clams and bake in oven.

# MARINATED CALAMARI

**Serves: 4**

1 large calamari (1/2 lb, 230 g)
 2 Tbsp white wine
 Pinch salt
 1/4 lemon
5 *shiso* (perilla) leaves
1/3 stalk celery
1/2 small onion

**Marinade**

1 Tbsp white wine vinegar
1 Tbsp virgin olive oil
Salt and pepper to taste

Mache(corn salad)

**1** Remove inside and skin of calamari. Cut into 1"(2.5 cm) rings. In boiling water, put wine, salt and lemon.

**2** Cook calamari in fragrant boiling water only briefly; drain and set aside.

**3** Mince *shiso* leaves. Slice onion and celery thinly. Blend marinade ingredients and add vegetables and calamari. Mix well as shown and refrigerate 1-2 hours. Serve garnished with mache leaves.

**Note:** When cooking calamari for marinating, remove from boiling water after 3-4 seconds as lingering heat cooks the rest.

**Variation:** Beef tongue can be a good substitute for calamari.

For rich flavor and good taste, put wine, salt and lemon.

**Don't overcook calamari.**

Mix well so calamari and vegetables are coated with marinade sauce.

# BAKED EGGPLANT

**Serves: 1**

1 eggplant
8 *shiso* (perilla) leaves
Mozzarella cheese
3/4 cup tomato sauce (see p.71)
Olive oil for frying

**1** Slice eggplant into 1/4"(6 mm) thicknesses. Peel, if desired. Heat olive oil in a skillet and fry eggplant slices until browned. Brush on olive oil. On bottom of a greased casserole, spread 4 Tbsp tomato sauce. Lay eggplant and spread tomato sauce again, as shown.

**2** Lay *shiso* leaves. Repeat layering.

**3** End with sliced mozzarella cheese. Bake in oven preheated to 350˚F(180˚C)) until surface is partially browned.

Spread tomato sauce and lay eggplant slices. Cover with tomato sauce again.

**Place *shiso* leaves and continue layering in the same order.**

**Top with sliced mozzarella cheese and bake in oven.**

# OCTOPUS PEPERONCINI

**Serves: 2**

1/4 lb (120 g)  boiled octopus
50 ml tomato sauce(see below)
1/4 cup olive oil
1/2 Tbsp minced garlic
1-2 pods dried chili
1/2 Tbsp minced parsley
Salt and pepper to taste

**1** Spread tomato sauce thinly over a serving plate.  Arrange thinly sliced octopus in rounds, starting from outside.
**2** In a skillet, fry minced garlic, red pepper and minced parsley in olive oil. Stir and cook over low heat until garlic is brownish, then remove from heat and pour over hot sauce over octopus .

**Note:** Crunchy fried garlic enhances the octopus's chewy texture and flavor.

Spread tomato sauce in the center of a plate. Lay octopus slices to cover sauce.

Fry garlic, dried red chili, and parsley in  olive oil. Pour over octopus while sauce is hot.

# EASY TOMATO SAUCE

## This tomato sauce is versatile as a base of many kinds of dishes

**Makes: 4 cups**

1/4 lb (120 g) tomato paste
3 lb (1350 g) canned whole
    tomatoes
2 onions, minced
1 clove garlic, minced
2 1/2 Tbsp all-purpose flour
90 ml olive oil
1 Tbsp beef buillon granules
2 bay leaves
1 dried red pepper

**1** Fry minced garlic and red pepper in olive oil, until garlic turns brownish.

**2** Add onion and contitue to fry, stirring constantly.

**3** Stir in flour, and cook carefully so as not to stick to the pot.
**Make a large batch and store in a glass jar. Keep refrigerated.**

**4** Add tomato paste and stir well. Add whole tomatoes and crush well.

**5** Add beef buillon granules and bay leaves, and reduce heat.

**6** Simmer about 30 minutes. If cooking over medium heat, be sure to stir occasionally.

Tough skin of bell peppers is easily removed by grilling over flame or in an toaster oven.

Blanch in cold water to peel blackened skin.

Cut vegetables into similar size, about 1"(2.5 cm) .

# CAPONATA

Simple yet nutritious dish you can cook at any time of the year.

**Serves: 4**

1 each, red and yellow bell pepper
2 small onions
1 eggplant
2 zucchinis
3 ripe tomatoes
1/2 clove garlic, minced
200 ml olive oil
Salt and pepper to taste

**1** Grill bell peppers on high heat, until blackened all over as shown.
**2** Blanch in cold water and remove blackened skin. Cut up.
**3** Cut zucchini half lengthwise, and then into 1"(2.5 cm) thick, half rounds.
**4** Cut onion into halves and then into 1"(2.5 cm) slices.

Remove core. Peel eggplant and cut into 1"(2.5 cm) thick rounds.
**5** In a deep saucepan, pour in ample olive oil and fry minced garlic briefly to release aroma. Add onion and stir-fry over low heat until transparent.
**6** Fry zucchini in a greased skillet, then add to the saucepan. Fry eggplant in skillet and add to saucepan (Use ample olive oil for eggplant as they absorb much oil). Cut up tomatoes and add to the saucepan. Cover and simmer 40-50 minutes over low heat, stirring lightly 2-3 times.

**Note:** All you have to do is just cut up and fry each vegetable before simmering together in their own juices. Shorten the final cooking time if you prefer some resilience in vegetables.

Split onion in two, remove cores, and slice.

First, stir-fry minced garlic, then onion over low heat.

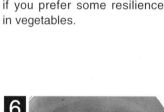

Add no water and cook in vegetables' own juices. Stir occasionally to avoid scorching.

# TUNA AND FUJILLI SALAD

Fujilli means " spool" in Italian.  As its spiral shape holds oil or sauce well,  it is mainly used in salads.

## Serves: 4

1/4 lb (120 g)  fujilli pasta
1 can (3 oz,90 g) tuna
1 each, red and yellow pepper
5 stalks fresh asparagus
1/2 lemon, squeezed
Salt and pepper to taste
Virgin olive oil
Mache (corn salad)

**1** Peel tough skin at base of asparagus as shown, and cut up. Deep-fry  until fresh green; drain on kitchen towel, sprinkle with salt and set aside to cool. Drain canned tuna and break into flakes.

**2** Grill peppers over flame or in a toaster oven until they scorch, then blanch into cold water to peel. Seed and cut up.

**3** Heat ample water to a boil, and cook fujilli until tender. Rinse under running water briefly and set aside to drain.

**4** In a bowl, mix asparagus, peppers, tuna and pasta with salt, pepper, virgin olive oil and lemon juice as shown.

**5** Refrigerate and garnish with mache(corn salad) or any salad greens.

Do not discard tough base of asparagus. Peel and cook longer than other parts.

Skinning bell peppers make a difference in texture and flavor. See opposite page (steps 1-2).

Cook pasta for salad a little further than"al dente". Blanch in cold water to stop cooking and to remove starch.

In a large bowl toss all ingredients with seasonings, and transfer into a serving bowl. Garnish with greens.

73

# CHICKEN LIVER SALAD

**Serves: 4**

7 oz(200g)  chicken liver
  Salt and pepper
  Vegetable oil
  1 Tbsp brandy or liquor
1/4 onion, minced
1 clove garlic, minces
1/3 cup olive oil
2 Tbsp wine vinegar
1 Tbsp whole grain mustard
Salt and pepper
Broccoli
Red-leaf lettuce
Iceberg lettuce
French baguette

**1** Rinse livers in cold water well and cut into bite-sized pieces. Sprinkle with salt and pepper, set aside.
**2** Grease a skillet and heat until smoke rises.  Saute liver pieces as shown,  pour in brandy or other liquor, and let it flame. Turn over several times and cook until "medium". Remove and set aside.
**3** Make garlic oil. Fry minced garlic in  olive oil over low heat, stirring constantly.
**4** Boil or steam broccoli. Tear lettuce leaves into bite size.
**5** In a bowl combine vinegar and mustard.  Add liver and vegetables. Sprinkle with salt and rub with your hand. Add pepper and rub again so flavor penetrates.
**6** Pour in garlic oil and toss well.
**7** Slice French baguette thinly and toast until crisp. Break into small pieces and add to salad as shown.  Serve immediately.

The key to success: Toss just before you serve .

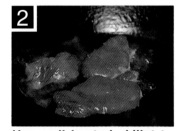

**Use well heated skillet to saute chicken liver to prevent scorching.**

**Prepare all ingredients and toss just before serving.**

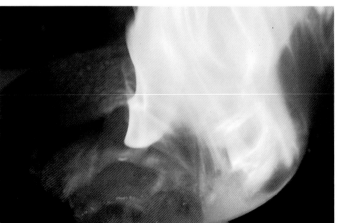

# ARUGULA AND AVOCADO SALAD

Easy but flavorful salad with an accent of Parmesiano Reggiano.

## Serves: 2

1-1 1/2 oz(30-40 g)  arugula
1/2 avocado
Olive oil
Wine vinegar
Salt and pepper to taste
Parmesiano Reggiano

**1** In a bowl, place cut-up avocado and arugula leaves cut into 2.

**2** Combine olive oil and wine vinegar at a ratio of 3:1 in a bottle. Shake well until blended as shown.

**3** Pour 1 1/2 Tbsp olive oil mixture into bowl. Sprinkle with salt and pepper and toss well.

**4** Slice Parmesiano Reggiano very thinly.  Transfer tossed greens onto a serving dish and place parmesiano on top. Serve at once.

Arugula, which is also called Rocket, imparts a unique fragrance resembling toasted sesame seeds and gives an accent to ordinary salads together with its pungency. It is also mixed with pastas or used as a garnish to various dishes.

Using a spoon, scoop out avocado and cut into bite-size pieces.

In a bottle or jar, mix olive oil and wine vinegar by shaking well.

Add arugula to bowl, and pour in 1 1/2 Tbsp dressing. Adjust taste with salt and pepper. Toss well.

Slice Parmesiano Reggiano very thinly, break into 2″ (5 cm) pieces and place on tossed salad.

# BLUEFISH WITH HERBAL SAUCE

Olive oil enhances the fragrance of herbs without adding a greasy touch.

## Serves: 5

5 fillets  bluefish or halibut
1/2 bunch  basil
2 Tbsp minced parsley
1/3 Tbsp garlic, minced
Dried oregano
Dried basil
50 ml olive oil
1 tomato
Salt and pepper
Mache(corn salad)

**1** Prepare fresh herbs.  Chop basil roughly as shown. Mince parsley and garlic as finely as possible.

**2** In a small bowl, combine fresh herbs, 35 ml of olive oil, dried oregano and basil.

**3** Sprinkle both sides of fish fillets with salt and pepper. Place on a baking dish and spoon on herb mixture.

**4** Cook in a preheated oven until done as shown.

**5** Heat 15 ml olive oil in a skillet, fry sliced  tomatoes and sprinkle with salt and pepper.

**6** Transfer onto a serving dish and top with fried tomatoes. Garnish with mache or other green sprouts and serve while hot.

**1**

Chop basil leaves roughly. Parsley and garlic should be minced finely.

**2**

Stir fresh and dry herbs with olive oil.

**3**

Spread herbal sauce on fish fillets using a spoon.

**4**

Cook in oven until done. Do not overcook. Serve garnished with sliced tomatoes.

Prepare vegetables by slicing onion and *shiitake*, and mincing parsley and garlic.

Stir-fry onion and *shiitake*. Combine with parsley, garlic, grated Parmesan cheese, and breadcrumbs.

# INVOLTINI DI MAIALE

## Serves: 5

10 thinly sliced pork roast
 Salt and pepper
 Rosemary, minced
1 small onion, thinly sliced
2 *shiitake* mushrooms
1/3 clove garlic, minced
1 Tbsp minced parsley
Vegetable oil
Butter
Grated Parmesan cheese
2 Tbsp breadcrumbs
All-purpose flour for dusting
Vegetable oil
1/4 cup red wine
1/4 cup brown sauce
2 Tbsp heavy cream

**1** Split onion into quarters and slice thinly. Cut *shiitake* in half, then into thin slices.
**2** Grease a skillet with vegetable oil and butter. Fry minced onion and *shiitake* until supple; transfer into a bowl. Mix with parsley, grated Parmesan cheese and breadcrumbs as shown. Divide mixture into 10.
**3** Lay pork slices on a cutting board. Sprinkle with salt, pepper and rosemary. Hold one portion mixture firmly with your fingers, place on an edge of pork, and start rolling as shown.
**4** Roll toward one direction, and change to the other direction in the middle as shown. Secure rolls "sewing" with toothpicks.
**5** Dust rolls with flour and cook in a preheated, greased skillet, secured ends down.
**6** Turn over and cook until done. Sprinkle with red wine, and stir in brown sauce and heavy cream. Remove toothpicks and serve hot.

Roll so stuffing will not bulge out: First, roll towards left (or right), closing right (or left) end.

Change direction to right (or left) in middle and roll up; secure with a toothpick.

Cook stuffed pork rolls secured ends down, so ends do not come off.

When both sides are cooked, add wine, brown sauce and cream.

# POULE DIABLE

Easy deviled chicken with crisp mustard topping. Decorate with balsamic vinegar.

## Serves: 2

1 chicken thigh
 Salt and pepper

**Marinade**
⎰ 1 tsp  minced garlic
⎟ 1 tsp cayenne pepper
⎟ Dash olive oil
⎱ 1 Tbsp mustard
Breadcrumbs
2 tsp minced parsley
Olive oil for frying
Balsamic vinegar

**1** Sprinkle chicken with salt and pepper. In a bowl, place minced garlic, cayenne pepper and olive oil, then add chicken. Rub with your hand as shown so flavors are absorbed.

**2** In a skillet, heat olive oil and saute over medium heat until skin is crisp. At this point, chicken does not have to be cooked completely since rest of cooking will be done in oven.

**3** On one surface spread mustard using a spoon as shown. Cover mustard with breadcrumbs, then sprinkle with parsley.

**4** In an oven preheated to 400 °F (200°C), cook chicken 5-6 minutes until surface is golden.

Rub minced garlic, cayenne pepper and olive oil onto chicken.

Fry over medium heat until skin is crisp and 80% cooked.

Spread mustard evenly on one side.

Cover mustard with breadcrumbs and sprinkle with minced parsley. Cook in oven 5-6 minutes.

# YELLOWTAIL NAPOLETANA

### Serves: 2

5 oz (150 g)  yellowtail or
   Pacific blue marlin fillets
 Salt and pepper
 All-purpose flour for dusting
3  calamari(3 oz,100 g), sliced
7-8  baby clams
7-8  black olives
1 tsp chopped anchovy
1 tsp oregano
1 tsp pepper
1 tsp minced garlic
1/3 cup tomato sauce (see
   p.71)
2 Tbsp white wine
Olive oil for frying

**1** Sprinkle fish fillets with salt and pepper. Lightly dust with all-purpose flour. Heat olive oil in a skillet and saute fish fillets over high heat. When slightly browned, turn over and cook other side.  Heat  olive oil in a skillet, and saute fish fillets over high heat. Turn over when lightly browned.

**2** In another skillet, fry minced garlic in olive oil until lightly browned. Add black olives, anchovy, oregano and pepper. Stir-fry clams and calamari. Pour in white wine, then cover at once.

**3** When clam shells are open, add fish fillets.

**4** Add tomato sauce.  Cook briefly until  thickened as shown.

**Note:** Be careful so as not to break or overcook yellowtail. It is ready when lightly browned.

Tomato sauce makes this seafood dish rich and voluminous. Use any white meat fish of your choice.

Saute dusted yellowtail over high heat, turning over once.

When clams and calamari are added, place a lid immediately.

When  clam  shells  are open, remove lid and add yellowtail.

Shake skillet back and forth and sideways so all ingredients are covered\ with  tomato  sauce quickly.

79

**Make scores on fish skin so surface does not shrink when sauteed.**

# SAUTEED SEA BASS

## Serves: 2
5 sea bass fillets
  Salt and pepper
  All-purpose flour for dusting
  Vegetable oil for frying
**Pesto**
  1/4 bunch parsley
  150 ml olive oil
  Salt and pepper to taste
**Garnishes**
  *Shiitake*, *shimeji*, and button
    mushrooms
  1 clove garlic, minced
  50 ml olive oil
  Salt and pepper
  Balsamic vinegar

**1** On each fillet of sea bass, make two scores as shown, and sprinkle with salt and pepper.
**2** Heat small amount of vegetable oil in a skillet. Dust only skin sides of fish with flour. Saute, skin side down. Keep heat low and cook slowly until skin becomes crisp.
**3** Turn over fish, turn off heat, and let it cook with remaining heat of skillet.
**4** Blend pesto ingredients in a blender or food processor.
**5** Cut up mushrooms. Heat olive oil and minced garlic in a skillet until aroma is released. Stir in mushrooms and adjust taste with salt, pepper and balsamic vinegar.
**6** On a serving plate arrange sea bass and mushrooms. Drizzle on pesto around them.

Subtly flavored fish with irresistibly crisp fish skin contrasts with garnish with a hint of vinegar. An ideal companion to a dry, white wine.

**Dust only skin side and saute over low heat until brown and almost heated through.**

**Turn over and turn off heat at once. Remaining heat will do the cooking.**

**This pesto enhances any white meat fish.**

Cut up vegetables and measure Parmesan cheese.

Fry vegetables in order: onion and carrot, then shiitake and pepper.

Deep-fry or saute split eggplant, skin side down. Keep oil at 350°F (180°C) or less and cook slowly.

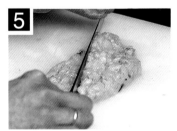

Do not damage eggplant skin when scraping out inside of eggplant.

Chop eggplant flesh finely before adding to filling.

Line souffle dish with eggplant skin, dark side down. Allow some extra to cover edges.

It is important to stir well until mixture is sticky.

Place filling and cover edges with extra skin. Cook and steam in an oven.

# STUFFED EGGPLANT

## Serves: 2

8 Japanese-type long eggplants  (or 2 regular eggplants)
3 cloves garlic, minced
1/2 each, onion and carrot, chopped
1/2 carrot, chopped
2 *shiitake* mushrooms, sliced
1/5 red bell pepper, diced
Vegetable oil for deep-frying
1/2 lb (230 g)  ground beef and pork
1 egg, beaten
1 oz (30 g)  grated Parmesan cheese
Dash allspice, salt and pepper
Tomato sauce (see p.71)
*Use leftover vegetable such as spring onion and mushroom.

**1** Prepare vegetables, cheese and egg for efficient cooking.
**2** Heat vegetable oil in a skillet, and fry vegetables as shown. Sprinkle with pinch of salt.
**3** Split eggplants in half lengthwise, and soak in water to remove harshness; wipe dry. Deep-fry until supple, skin side down turning once.
**4** Using a spoon, scrape out inside of eggplant. Slide spoon sideways and do not break skin.
**5** Chop inside of eggplant as shown and add to **2**.
**6** Line a souffle dish with eggplant skin, as shown.
**7** Using your fingers, stir cooked vegetables and ground meat with salt, pepper and allspice. Stir well until sticky. Stir in grated Parmesan cheese and beaten egg.
**8** Fill souffle dish meat mixture. Cover edges with extended skin. Pour hot water to a baking tray of preheated 350°F (180°C) oven. Cook and steam 30-40 minutes. Unmold and place on a serving plate, and serve with tomato sauce.

# BEEF BOURGUIGNON

**Serves: 2**

1 lb (450 g) chuck steak
3 1/3 oz (100 g) piece lean
    bacon

**Marinade**
1 cup red wine
1/3 cup red wine vinegar
1/2 onion
1-2 carrots

1/2 stalk celery
1 clove garlic, crushed
1 sprig thyme
1 bay leaf
Vegetable oil for frying
All-purpose flour for dusting
2 beef bouillon cubes
1 Tbsp blueberry jam

**Note 1:** Marinate meat and vegetables in wine, vinegar and herbs overnight in refrigerator.
**Note 2:** Step **10**, bring to a boil over high heat. Remove scum and excess fat carefully and reduce heat.
**Note 3:** Stir in jam just before serving.

**1** Trim away excess fat from beef.

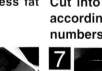
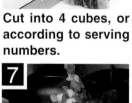
**2** Cut into 4 cubes, or according to serving numbers.

**3** Dice vegetables and bacon into 3/8" (1cm). Crush celery before dicing.

**4** Marinate meat and vegetables overnight in an acid-proof container.

**5** Marinade has been absorbed into meat and vegetables.

**6** Drain through a strainer and separate beef pieces. Reserve marinade.

**7** Fry bacon and vegetables over medium heat until tender. Add to saucepan.

**8** In ample vegetable oil, saute dusted beef.

**9** Brown all sides so flavor will not be released when simmered. Add to saucepan.

**10** Add water to saucepan, just to cover ingredients. Cover and simmer 3-4 hours.

Prepared bacon and vegetables. From bottom clockwise: garlic, celery, bacon, carrot, and onion.

Cook and stir in right order, over low heat.

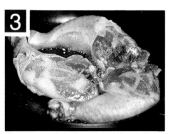

Saute chicken skin side down over high heat, so surface is crisp.

# BRAISED CHICKEN AND PRAWNS

## Serves: 5

5 whole chicken thighs
 1 Tbsp vegetable oil
5 whole prawns, deveined
1/2 onion, chopped
1/2 carrot, chopped
1/2 stalk celery, chopped
2 cloves garlic, chopped
1 2/3 oz bacon, chopped

**Cooking Sauce**
 200 ml white wine
 2 Tbsp tomato paste
 2 bouillon cubes
 1 bay leaf
Olive oil for frying
Salt and pepper to taste
All-purpose flour for dusting

**Be sure to use whole prawns since their heads give the key flavor to this deeply flavored dish.**

❶Prepare vegetables and bacon by chopping finely as shown.
❷Fry garlic in olive oil until aroma is released. Add bacon, then vegetables. Cook and stir over low heat, until supple.
❸Sprinkle salt and pepper on chicken thighs, and dust with flour. Heat vegetable oil and saute chicken skin side down over high heat.
❹Turn over and cook until crisp. This coating will keep chicken juice inside when simmered.
❺In same skillet vegetables have been fried, place chicken and add cooking sauce ingredients. Add some water and cook over low heat. Add prawns and skim foam. Simmer 20-30 minutes.

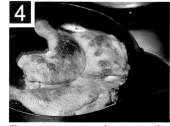

Turn over and saute in same manner.

Add chicken to vegetables and simmer in cooking sauce. Lastly add prawns.

# PIZZA CAPRICCIOSA & FOCCACCIA

Italy's masterpiece of snack, pizza has two styles — Capriccioza is baked with sauce and toppings, whereas Foccaccia is baked alone and served with unbaked toppings.

See page 86 for recipes.

# PIZZA DOUGH

**1** In a small bowl, mix dried yeast, sugar and lukewarm water.

**2** Cover with plastic wrap and let stand in a warm place 10 minutes, or until bubbly.

**3** In a large bowl, mix all purpose flour and salt. Add bubbly yeast mixture with milk and olive oil.

**4** Knead well until dough is not sticky.

**5** Knead on a smooth surface using both hands, occasionally flinging against surface.

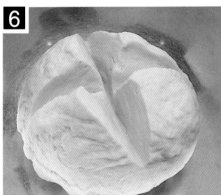

**6** Form into a ball and cut a deep crisscross score. Cover with plastic wrap and let rise 40 minutes at room temperature.

## Makes: 8 sheets

4 cups all-purpose flour
1/3 oz(10 g) active dry yeast
1/2 Tbsp sugar
135 ml milk
40 ml olive oil
1/2 Tbsp salt
135 ml lukewarm water

**1** In a small bowl, combine yeast, sugar and lukewarm water.
**2** Cover and let rest in a warm place 10 minutes until bubbly.
**3** In a large bowl, combine flour and salt. Pour in yeast mixture, milk and olive oil.
**4** Mix well until dough doesn't stick to your hand.
**5** Turn onto a smooth surface such as a cutting board, and knead vigorously. Throw onto surface several times so as to give a resilience.
**6** When elastic enough, shape into a bowl and make deep scores as shown. Cover and let rise 40 minutes.

●**Shaping pizza dough**
(see overleaf))
**7** Let rise as shown by resting 40 minutes at room temperature.
**8** Knead well so as to release extra gas.
**9** Shape into a ball again, and divide into 8 balls, squeezing with your hand. Cover until use.
**10** Take 1 portion in your hand, and place on a dry surface.
**11** Roll out into about 10"(25 cm) diam round.
**12** Prick with a fork.

**Note:** In order to let dough rise, place it in a warm place such as a bathroom. However, if the mixture is not bubbling, it is not fermented enough, and it will not blend with flour well. Do it all over again.

# SHAPING PIZZA DOUGH

**7** Let rise as shown by resting 40 minutes at room temperature.

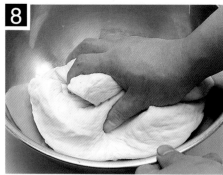

**8** Using your palm, knead well so as to release air from inside.

**9** Between your thumb and fingers, hold dough and squeeze out into a ball. Form 8 balls.

**10** Press one portion flat using your fingers.

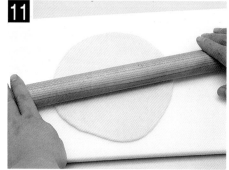

**11** Turn onto a cutting board and roll out from center outward.

**12** Prick with a fork to prevent swelling while being baked.

# PIZZA CAPRICCIOSA

1 portion pizza dough (see p.85)
Tomato sauce (see p.71)
Oregano
1 egg
**Toppings** (octopus, bacon, onion, tomato, *shimeji* mushrooms, eggplant, zucchini, black olives and mozzarella cheese)

**1** Heat tomato sauce until thickened, and stir in oregano.
**2** Roll out pizza dough to 10" (25 cm) in diameter. Spread tomato sauce and place thinly sliced mozzarella cheese.
**3** Slice all topping ingredients and arrange on dough. Drop egg onto center, and sprinkle with oregano.
**4** In 425°F (250°C) oven, bake 5-8 minutes.

**2** Line a baking dish with rolled out dough, and spread thickened tomato sauce.

**3** Place toppings evenly, and drop egg onto center. Sprinkle with oregano. Bake 5-8 minutes.

# PIZZA FOCCACCIA

1 portion pizza dough (see p.85)
Virgin olive oil
Salt and pepper
**Toppings** ( prosciutto, tomato, arugula, Parmisiano Reggiano)
Red wine vinegar
Minced parsley

**1** Preheat oven to 425°F (250°C), and bake rolled out pizza dough 2-3 minutes until surface is completely dry, but not browned.
**2** Sprinkle baked dough with virgin olive oil, salt and pepper. Place arugula and sliced tomato. Pour over red wine vinegar.
**3** Cut into 6 portions. Place thinly sliced prosciutto and shaved Parmisiano Reggiano. Sprinkle with minced parsley.

**1** Remove from oven when dough is dry on surface but not browned.

**2** Sprinkle with olive oil, salt and pepper. Place toppings and pour over vinegar.

# PIZZA CALZONE

1 portion pizza dough (see p.85)
3 1/3 oz (100 g) canned meat sauce
2/3 oz (20 g) fresh mozzarella cheese

**1** Over rolled out dough, prick with a fork and turn over. On upper half, place meat sauce and sliced fresh mozzarella cheese as shown.
**2** Bring up lower half of dough so its edges are 1/2"(1.5 cm) inside upper edges.
**3** Fold down upper edges to seal.
**4** Using a fork, secure edges as shown. In 425°F (250°C) oven, bake 5 minutes.

**Note:** The key to success: Bake quickly in well-preheated oven. If baked long in low heat, the dough will become tough to chew.

Ideal party food. Enjoy a variety of stuffings.

Place meat sauce and cheese on upper half of dough.

Fold up lower half, to 1/2 " (1.5 cm) inside upper edge.

Fold down upper edges to secure.

Press along edges using tip of fork.

# SPAGHETTI WITH DRIED SARDINE

Simple yet flavorful pasta enhanced with crisp fried sardine.

### Serves: 1

3 1/3 oz(100 g)  dried thin spaghetti
  1 1/3 Tbsp  salt
1 oz (30g)  dried baby sardine (*chirimenjako*)
1 stalk scallion
1 Tbsp minced garlic
1 pod dried chili pepper
100 ml olive oil
1/2 Tbsp butter

**1** Add salt to 1200 ml boiling water, and cook spaghetti until "al dente".
**2** Fry minced garlic and sliced chili pepper in olive oil as shown.
**3** When garlic pieces turn golden, add dried baby sardine and fry until crisp.
**4** Reduce heat to low and add cooked spaghetti and butter. Mix well.
**5** Transfer onto a serving dish, and garnish generously with sliced scallion.

**1** Cook spaghetti in heavily salted boiling water just until "al dente".

**2** Fry garlic and chili in olive oil until garlic turns golden.

**3** Add dried baby sardine and fry until crisp.

**4** Reduce heat and add spaghetti and butter. Stir quickly and serve hot.

# SPAGHETTI AL PEPERONCINO & VARIATIONS

## Serves: 1

3 1/3 oz (100 g) spaghetti
1 clove garlic, sliced
1 pod dried chili pepper
30 ml olive oil

### SPAGHETTI AL PEPERONCINO WITH TOMATOES
**Add:**

1 large tomato (canned), cut up

### SPAGHETTI AL PEPERONCINO WITH *SHISO*
**Add:**

10 or 1 package *shiso* (perilla) leaves, chopped

**1** In a skillet, heat olive oil and fry sliced garlic. Tilt skillet as shown so garlic slices are covered with oil. Tear chili pepper into halves and remove seeds.

**2** When garlic turns brownish, stir in chili pepper, and remove from heat immediately.

**3** Heat 3L water to a boil and add 2 1/2 Tbsp salt. Cook spaghetti till al dente, drain and add to skillet. Stir quickly.

### SPAGHETTI AL PEPERONCINO WITH TOMATOES
Cook garlic and chili in same manner as left, and add cut-up tomatoes. Add cooked spaghetti and mix well.

### SPAGHETTI AL PEPERONCINO WITH *SHISO*
Cook in same manner as left, mix with cooked spaghetti, and stir in chopped *shiso* leaves. Serve immediately.

Once you have mastered basic Peperoncino, myriads of variations are possible. Create your own and enjoy!

**2**

**3**

**Do not brown garlic. Tilt skillet so oil covers garlic slices.**

**When garlic slices are slightly browned, add chili and remove from heat at once.**

**Add spaghetti cooked al dente, and mix quickly so spaghetti is evenly coated.**

# PENNE GORGONZOLA

**Serves: 1**

2 2/3 oz (80 g) penne
1 2/3 oz (50 g) gorgonzola
   cheese
2/3 cup heavy cream
Parsley, minced
Salt and pepper to taste

**1** In a saucepan, heat heavy cream and gorgonzola cheese over low heat until cheese melts and sauce thickens for richer flavor.

**2** Cook penne slightly harder than usual, and add to pan.

**3** When sauce is thick enough to coat penne, add minced parsley, salt and pepper. Stir well so penne is coated evenly.

**Note:** Stir the sauce constantly over low heat as it scorches easily.

# EGG AND CHEESE RISOTTO

**Serves: 1**

100 ml rice
Olive oil
2 oz(60 g) bacon, diced
1 small potato diced
2 oz(60 g) fresh mozzarella
   cheese
2/3 oz (20 g) Parmigiano
   Reggiano
Parsley, minced
1 egg, beaten
1 Tbsp butter

**1** In a large saucepan, heat ample water, a few drops olive oil, and rice. Cook until almost tender about 15 minutes. Cut fresh mozzarella cheese into 3/8"(1 cm) dices and let stand at room temperature.

**2** In a skillet, heat olive oil and fry diced bacon until crisp.

**3** Deep-fry potato and drain.

**4** In a large bowl, put everything and stir well until the mixture develops a sticky consistency.

Make a rich sauce by thickening melted cream and gorgonzola cheese.

Add cooked penne and continue to cook until condensed.

Cook rice in ample water with olive oil and drain before completely tender.

Mix rice with all other ingredients until gooey threads are seen.

# SAUSAGE AND ONION CONFURE SANDWICH

### Serves: 5

2 onions, sliced
1/2 each red and yellow pepper
2 Tbsp olive oil
1 Tbsp butter
100 ml balsamic vinegar
100 ml olive oil
1 clove garlic, minced
1 sprig thyme
1 lb (450 g) sausages
Chicory leaves
1 French baguette

**1** In a skillet heat olive oil and butter. Fry sliced onion over low heat.

**2** When onions are browned as shown, stir in balsamic vinegar; set aside.

**3** Cut up peppers. In another skillet, fry garlic in olive oil and add peppers.

**4** Split sausages lengthwise into halves and add to skillet.

**5** Split French baguette lengthwise into halves, and toast only surfaces lightly. On bottom half, spread browned onion as shown.

**6** Place sausage halves, peppers, and chicory leaves. Place other half of French baguette.

**Note:** Olive oil is recommendable for frying vegetables since other vegetable oils will leave some kind of greasiness in your mouth. Olive oil does not give heaviness even if it is used generously.

Fry thinly sliced onions in olive oil and butter, over low heat.

Stir constantly with a wooden spatula until onions turn dark brown.

Fry garlic first to release aroma. Add chopped peppers.

Add sausages cut into halves and cook just until heated through.

Over toasted baguette, spread onion confure.

Place sausages and vegetables and top with remaining half baguette.

# GLOSSARY

*-age* —Suffix meaning "deep-frying" or "deep-fried dish". *Agemono*.
*Kara-age* is dusted with plain or seasoned flour before frying, whereas
*Kaki-age* is a mixed *tempura* which is dipped in a batter and deep-fried.

*-an* —Suffix meaning "thick broth"; usually a clear sauce poured over as a glaze.

**antipasti** —Plural form of "antipasto". Appetizers or first courses in Italian cuisine.

**bamboo shoot** —*Takenoko*. One of the most common ingredients in Asian cooking. Fresh bamboo shoot is a spring delicacy, but it is boiled and canned to be available all through the year.

*buta* —Both pork and pig are called *buta* in Japanese, but *buta-niku* is used when one wishes to emphasize that it is pork.

**caponata** —A typical vegetable stew of Italy. Ratatouille in French cooking.

*chawan-mushi* —Savory egg custard steamed(*mushi*) in a cup(*chawan*). Beaten(but not whisked) eggs are blended with seasoned *dashi* stock and tiny chewable ingredients such as ginkgo nuts and chicken, then steamed until set.

*chirimenjako* —Dried baby sardines.

**cloud ear mushroom** —Crunchy black mushroom usually sold in dried form. It is soaked in hot water until softened, before being cooked with other ingredients.

**confure** —Confire in French. Vegetables or fruit marinated in sugar or vinegar for the preserving purpose.

**cucumber** —Japanese-type cucumbers are smaller in size and have thinner skin and less seeds, and therefore need no peeling or seeding.

*daikon* **radish** —Large white radish, 10"-20"(25-50 cm) long and 3"-4"(7.5-10cm) thick. This radish is a must for Japanese tables and is eaten in numerous ways such as pickling, simmering, and frying, besides being grated to make condiments.

*dashi* —A basic stock widely used in Japanese cooking. *Kombu* (giant kelp) and *katsuobushi* (dried bonito flakes) are cooked briefly in boiling water, and then removed to make a clear broth. Today busy wives prefer to use powdered or granulated form sold in jars or sachets. *Soba-tsuyu*, or noodle dipping sauce, is made of *dashi* stock, *mirin*, *sake*, sugar and soy sauce, and makes a good cooking sauce for various simmered dishes.

**eggplant** —Japanese-type eggplants are smaller in size and have tender texture and skin. Be careful about the amount if using the western type.

*enokidake* **mushroom** —White mushrooms with tiny caps and long, narrow stems, cultivated in the same condition as the common button mushrooms. They have a delicate flavor and pleasant crispness.

**Fujilli** —Spool-shaped macaroni, often used in salads.

*furofuki* —As indicated in the name "*furo* (bath or steam bath)", this is a steaming hot, winter dish of vegetable (mainly *daikon*), simmered until fork-tender and eaten with thick sauces.

**ginger root** —Ginger is used only in fresh form in Asian cooking. When choosing, look for firm rhizomes.

*hiyayakko* —Chilled *tofu*, known as the typical and easiest way of serving *tofu* in summer. Condiments such as scallions and grated ginger accompany it as well as soy sauce.

*kabu* —Japanese-type turnip which has tenderer and smoother texture compared to western type. It cooks fast and creates a delicate flavor when cooked or pickled.

**kaki-age** —A kind of *tempura*. A few kinds of thinly sliced ingredients are mixed and gathered(*kaki*) with *tempura* batter, and deep-fried. See "*-age*".

**kaku-ni** —Meat or fish stewed in cube form.

**kamaboko** —Fish cake. White meat fish paste is heaped on a piece of wood, and steamed to make a resilient cake.

**katsuobushi** —Dried bonito shavings now sold in small pouches. This is the main ingredient for making *dashi* stock, but is also used as a garnish or topping to add flavor to various Japanese dishes.

**kimchee** —Korean word meaning "pickles". Spicy and sour pickled Chinese cabbage eaten daily in Korea.

**kochu jang** —Korean hot sauce made from barley and soy bean malts. Comes in a jar and keeps indefinitely is refrigerated.

**kombu** kelp —Dried giant kelp mainly used to make *dashi* stock. It is cut into desired size with scissors and added to cold water.

**konnyaku** —Sold as "yam cake", this is a jelly made of cooked gelatinous mountain yam. It became popular in Japan also as a health food because it contains no calories but lots of dietary fiber.

**kuzukiri** —Transparent noodle style jelly made of kudzu. High quality kudzu starch is cooked and cut into long strips when cooled and set. Usually sold in dried form and needs parboiling until it reaches desired softness.

**lotus root** —*Renkon*. Thick rhizome with tubular hollows which run through the length of it. Loved for its crunchiness and attractive shape. When parboiling, add some vinegar to water in order to prevent discoloring. Delicious in *tempura*, simmered or sauteed dishes.

**mentaiko** —Chili-flavored, heavily salted cod roe. It has become very popular in Japan since the introduction from Korea, and is served as a part of everyday meal. Other than being eaten on its own, it also makes great dressings for seafood or vegetable salads.

**mentsuyu** —*Soba* soup base. Bottled *mentsuyu* is available in Japanese food section.

**mirin** —A thick, sweet wine made from glutinous rice, used primarily in cooking. It gives rich flavor and glaze to food such as in *teriyaki*.

**miso** —Fermented soybean paste. It is a must-have seasoning in most households in Japan. Besides being used for making *miso* soups and dressings, it is used as a pickling bed or a dip. There are numerous types including yellow, brown and dark brown in color and sweet to salty in flavor.

**mitsuba** —Trefoil, a member of the parsley family. This herb has a delicate fragrance, somewhere between sorrel and celery, and is used to accent many Japanese dishes.

**mochi** —Rice cake. Cooked glutinous rice is pounded until soft and sticky, and then formed into cakes. *Mochi* originated as a form of rice for preservation to be served on special occasions. It is, however, now sold in packaged portions and eaten all through the year.

**myoga** —A young, pinkish fresh ginger flower head, treasured as a summer herb. It has a distinctive fragrance which enhances various salads, soups and pickles. Also good for *tempura*.

**nameko mushroom** —Tiny, orange to reddish brown mushroom with glutenous cap. The jelly-like substance that covers the brown cap is said to protect the walls of your stomach from strong acid or salt irritation. However, *nameko* mushroom has been loved for its smooth touch and delicate flavor, rather than for its health effect. Available in cans or bags.

**namool** —Name of a Korean dish meaning "assorted vegetables". Usually seasoned with sesame oil, soy sauce, grated garlic, sesame seeds and chili powder.

**natto** —Fermented soybeans with a sticky texture and strong aroma, which westerners may take some time to acquire a taste. It is a great source of protein and vitamin K.

**nikujaga** —One of the best selling small dishes in *izakaya*. *Niku* (meat) and *jaga* (potatoes) are simmered in sweet-salty sauce.

**nori** seaweed —Known as a wrapper for *sushi*, this edible blackish seaweed comes in dried thin sheets. It needs to be stored in an airtight container.

**renkon** —Lotus root.

**rice vinegar** —This vinegar has a milder flavor than most western varieties. Lightness and subtle sweetness are the characteristics of this vinegar. Essential for tossing cooked rice with when making *sushi* rice.

**rice wine** —*Sake* (below).

**sake** —Rice wine. Known as a popular Japanese beverage, *sake* also plays a major role in Japanese cooking. It is used to remove unpleasant odors of meat or fish, and to soften meat or vegetables quickly, as well as giving a delicate flavor to most dishes.

**sashimi** —Sliced fresh fish served "au naturel". Tuna *sashimi* is most popular, but in *izakaya*, *sashimi* is often served as an assortment of several kinds of fish and shellfish.

**sesame oil** —An essential ingredient for most Asian cooking. Sesame oil has a nutty fragrance and is mainly used to add flavor, rather than for deep- or stir-frying foods.

**shiitake** mushroom —A large, dark brown mushroom used in both fresh and dried forms. It has a distinctive aroma and smoothness, and is used in many Japanese dishes.

**shimeji** mushroom —A greyish white mushroom that grows with overlapping oyster-shell-shaped caps. It has more flavor and less fragrance than *shiitake* mushroom.

**shinjo** —Delicately flavored, soft but resilient seafood cake served as an appetizer. Ground seafood such as shrimp or white-meat fish is blended with *yamaimo*, egg whites and *dashi*, and then steamed or deep-fried. Chicken is sometimes used to substitute seafood.

**shirako** —Milt of codfish or globefish, treasured for the delicate flavor, although milt of other fish usually do not please your taste buds.

**shirataki** —Sold as "yam noodles", opaque filaments made from *konnyaku* yam. *Shirataki* is a must for *sukiyaki*, because it absorbs flavors well and the texture is smooth and slippery. Parboiling is often necessary to remove lime substance.

**shiso** —Perilla leaves in green or purple-red color. This herb is related to the mint family and has a pleasant aroma. Green *shiso* is usually used for cooking or as a condiment for *sashimi* platters.

**somen** —Japanese extra fine noodles made of wheat flour. They cook in only a couple of minutes and plunged into ice-cold water to prevent overcooking. They are then drained and served in light *soba- tsuyu* sauce. *Somen* is popular in Japan as a summer treat.

**takenoko** —Bamboo shoot.

**takuan** —Pickled *daikon* radish, yellow or whitish in color. *Takuan* is loved for the crispness and is available in plastic bags.

**tarako** —Codfish roe, usually salted for preserving purpose. *Tarako* is one of the most popular salted fish eggs as well as *ikura*, which is favored like caviar.

**toban jang** —Chinese seasoning known as hot bean paste. It is made from soy beans, chili peppers and sometimes garlic, and comes in jars or cans.

*tofu* —Soybean curd. *Tofu* is rich in proteins, vitamins and minerals, and is entirely free of cholesterol because of the low content of saturated fat. *Tofu* cakes should be kept in water, which should be changed daily.

*umeboshi* —Pickled Japanese plum. *Umeboshi* is another health food of Japan, and it has long been used as a tonic, not only because it helps digestion but also keeps the intestinal tract clear. *Umeboshi* paste makes a piquant dressing for seafood salads and is available in tubes.

*uni* —Sea urchin roe, usually served fresh as *sushi* or *sashimi*. Cooked *uni* seasoned with *sake* is called *neri-uni* and is available in jars. It is convenient to be used as a base of sauces for various food.

*yamaimo* —Mountain yam. There are two types; *yamatoimo* and *nagaimo* (see p.14). To prevent discoloring, *yamaimo* is soaked a little while in vinegared water after it is peeled.

*yamatoimo* —One of the two kinds of *yamaimo* (above).

*udo* —A vegetable that heralds spring with its special fragrance and crisp texture. *Udo* can be substituted with thinly sliced celery.

*wasabi* —Japanese green horseradish, most familiar in the West as a mound of pungent green paste served with *sushi* and *sashimi*. Originally, the rhizome is grated finely, however, nowadays *wasabi* is available in tubes or packed in small portions. It is proved that *wasabi* has sterilizing properties.

# INDEX

# ACKNOWLEDGMENTS

Cooking Staff:  Kunihiko Hashimoto
                Satoshi Yagi
                Akinobu Mori
                Tadashi Shimada
                Seikichi Sawaguchi
                Okusun Paku
                Meijin Han
Photographers: Hidetoshi Kamata
                Noriaki Moriya
                Yoshihiko Koshizuka
Translator: Yoko Ishiguro
Project Editors: Studio Dunk
English Editor:Mieko Baba